HOLT
1
SPANISH

¡Ven conmigo!®

Student Make-Up Assignments

HOLT, RINEHART AND WINSTON

A Harcourt Classroom Education Company

Austin · New York · Orlando · Atlanta · San Francisco · Boston · Dallas · Toronto · London (tl), Index Stock; (c), Network Productions/Index Stock; (br), Digital Imagery ® © 2003

¡VEN CONMIGO! is a trademark licensed to Holt, Rinehart and Winston, registered in the United States of America and/or other jurisdictions.

Printed in the United States of America

ISBN 0-03-065901-9

1 2 3 4 5 6 7   066   05 04 03 02 01

Table of Contents

ANSWERS

Spanish 1 ¡Ven conmigo!

To the Teacher

The blackline masters in this ancillary will help you keep track of the instructional material covered in a school year, so that you can give make-up information to students who missed class.

The first section of the book is a Diagnostic Table. In the first column of the table is a list of all the major presentations that make up the building blocks of the **Capítulo:** the functional expressions, the grammar, and the vocabulary. The activities listed in the other four columns are correlated to the **Más práctica gramatical** in the *Pupil's Edition,* the **Cuaderno de actividades,** the **Cuaderno de grámatica,** and the **Interactive CD-ROM Tutor.** This table, which gives you an overview of the presentations and opportunities for practice, it can also be used as a global reference for students who need extra practice in problem areas.

The second section of the book contains the Student Make-Up Assignments Checklists. These blackline masters (one for each **paso** of the *Pupil's Edition)* can be photocopied and given to students as make-up assignments. On the left-hand side of each blackline master is a list of the presentations in each **paso.** If students missed a specific presentation (or presentations), the checklist tells them what activities they can do in the **Más práctica gramatical** in the *Pupil's Edition,* the **Cuaderno de actividades,** the **Cuaderno de grámatica,** or the **Interactive CD-ROM Tutor** to practice the material they missed when they were absent from class.

The third section of the book contains Alternative Quizzes that can be given to students who were absent from class when the regular Grammar and Vocabulary Quiz (Quiz A in the Testing Program) was given. The Alternative Quizzes could also be used in a different way: You can give both quizzes in the regular class, alternating rows, for example, so that students are not tempted to glance at their neighbor's paper.

The Alternative Quizzes were carefully built to reflect the same weight and level of difficulty as the regular quizzes, so that you can be assured that two students who take different versions of the quiz feel that they have been tested equally.

Diagnostic Information

The activities listed in this table are taken from the **Más práctica gramatical** in the *Pupil's Edition*, the **Cuaderno de actividades**, the **Cuaderno de gramática**, and the **CD-ROM Tutor**. They provide students with extra practice in problem areas.

Gramática = white background; **Vocabulario** = light gray; **Así se dice** = dark gray

CAPÍTULO 1	Más práctica gramatical	Cuaderno de gramática	Cuaderno de actividades	Interactive CD-ROM Tutor
Saying hello and goodbye		Act. 1, p. 1		
Introducing people and responding to an introduction	Act 2, p. 38	Act. 2, p. 1		
Diacritic marks	Act. 1, p. 38	Acts. 3–5, p. 2		
Asking how someone is and saying how you are	Act. 2, p. 38	Acts. 6–7, p. 3	Acts. 5–7, pp. 5–6	Acts. 1–2, CD 1
Subject pronouns **tú** and **yo**	Act. 3, p. 38	Acts. 8–10, p. 4		
Asking and saying how old someone is	Act. 7, p. 41			
Numbers from 0 to 30	Act. 4, p. 39	Acts. 11–13, p. 5		Act. 3, CD 1
Singular forms of the verb **ser**	Act. 5, p. 39	Act. 14, p. 6		
Asking where someone is from and saying where you're from	Act. 6, p. 40		Acts. 11–13, p. 8	
Forming questions with question words	Act. 7, p. 41	Act. 15, p. 6		Act. 4, CD 1
Talking about likes and dislikes	Acts. 8–9, p. 41			
Vocabulario: Sports	Acts. 8–9, p. 41	Acts. 16–17, p. 7		Act. 6, CD 1
Nouns and definite articles	Act. 9, p. 41	Acts. 18–20, p. 8		
CAPÍTULO 2	Más práctica gramatical	Cuaderno de gramática	Cuaderno de actividades	Interactive CD-ROM Tutor
Vocabulario: School supplies	Acts. 1–5, pp. 66–67	Acts. 1–2, p. 9	Act. 3, p. 14	Act. 1, CD 1
Talking about what you want and need	Acts. 3, 5, pp. 66–67			
Making nouns plural	Act. 2, p. 66	Acts. 5–6, p. 11		
Indefinite articles (**un, una, unos, unas**)	Acts. 3, 4, 7, 8, pp. 10, 12	Acts. 7–8, p. 12		Act. 2, CD 1
Personal pronouns **él** and **ella**	Acts. 4–5, p. 67	Acts. 9–10, p. 13		
Vocabulario: Debora's room	Act. 6, p. 67	Acts. 11–12, p. 14		Act. 3, CD 1
Describing the contents of your room	Act. 6, p. 67			
Agreement of **mucho** and **¿cuánto?** with nouns	Act. 7, p. 68	Act. 13, p. 15	Acts. 11–13, pp. 18–19	Act. 4, CD 1
Talking about what you need and want to do	Acts. 8–9, pp. 68–69		Acts. 14–17, pp. 20–21	Act. 5, CD 1
Vocabulario: Things you need to do and want to do	Act. 9, p. 69	Act. 14, p. 16		
The verbs **comprar, poner, conocer,** and **ir**		Act. 15, p. 16		
Vocabulario: Numbers from 31 to 199	Act. 10, p. 69	Acts. 16–17, p. 17		Act. 6, CD 1

CAPÍTULO 3	Más práctica gramatical	Cuaderno de gramática	Cuaderno de actividades	Interactive CD-ROM Tutor
Vocabulario: Names of classes	Acts. 2, 4, pp. 100–101	Acts. 1–2, p. 18		Act. 3, CD 1
The plural forms of definite articles	Act. 1, p. 100	Acts. 3–5, p. 19		
Talking about classes and sequencing events	Acts. 2, 4, pp. 100–101			
Así se dice Telling time	Acts. 2–3, pp. 100–101			Act. 1, CD 1
Gramática Telling time	Acts. 2–3, pp. 100–101	Acts. 6–7, p. 20	Acts. 7–8, p. 28	Act. 2, CD 1
Telling at what time something happens	Acts. 3–4, p. 100			
Vocabulario: Times of the day	Act. 3, p. 101	Acts. 8–9, p. 21		
The usage of the preposition **de**	Act. 5, p. 102	Acts. 10–11, p. 22		
Talking about being late or in a hurry			Acts. 11–12, pp. 30–31	Act. 4, CD 1
Describing people and things	Acts. 6–7, pp. 102–103			
The verb **ser**	Act. 7, p. 103	Acts. 12–13, p. 23		
Vocabulario: Adjectives	Acts. 6–7, pp. 102–103	Acts. 14–16, p. 24		Act. 6, CD 1
Adjective Agreement	Act. 7, p. 103	Act. 17, p. 25	Acts. 16–17, pp. 33–34	
Talking about things you like and explaining why	Act. 8, p. 103			Act. 5, CD 1
Vocabulario: Things you like or dislike	Acts. 6, 8, pp. 102, 103	Acts. 18–19, p. 26		
Tag questions			Act. 14, p. 32	
CAPÍTULO 4	Más práctica gramatical	Cuaderno de gramática	Cuaderno de actividades	Interactive CD-ROM Tutor
Talking about what you like to do		Acts. 1–2, p. 27	Act. 3, p. 38	
Vocabulario: Chores and pastimes	Acts. 1–3, pp. 128–129			Act. 1, CD 1
Present tense of regular **-ar** verbs	Act. 1, p. 128	Acts. 3–4, p. 28		Act. 2, CD 1
Discussing what you and others do during free time	Acts. 1–3, pp. 128–129	Acts. 5–6, p. 29		
Vocabulario: Activities in your free time	Acts. 1–3, pp. 128–129	Act. 7, p. 29		
The usage of the preposition **con**	Act. 2, p. 128	Act. 8, p. 30		
The relative pronoun **que**	Act. 3, p. 129	Act. 9, p. 30		
Telling where people and things are	Acts. 4–5, p. 129			Act. 3, CD 1
The verb **estar**	Acts. 4–6, pp. 129–130	Acts. 10–11, p. 31		Act. 4, CD 1
Vocabulario: Directions	Acts. 4–5, p. 129	Acts. 12–13, p. 32	Acts. 8–9, pp. 41–42	
Subject pronouns	Acts. 5–7, pp. 129–130	Acts. 14–16, p. 33		
Talking about where you and others go during free time	Acts. 7–9, pp. 130–131			
The verb **ir**	Act. 7, p. 130	Acts. 17–18, p. 34	Acts. 11–12, p. 44	Act. 5, CD 1
Vocabulario: The days of the week	Acts. 8–9, p. 131	Acts. 19–20, p. 35		Act. 6, CD 1
The usage of the definite article and the days of the week	Act. 8, p. 131	Acts. 21–23, p. 36		

Spanish 1 ¡Ven conmigo!

CAPÍTULO 5	Más práctica gramatical	Cuaderno de gramática	Cuaderno de actividades	Interactive CD-ROM Tutor
Discussing how often you do things	Acts. 1, 2, p. 160			Act. 1, CD 2
Negation	Act. 2, p. 160	Acts. 1–3, pp. 37–38	Acts. 3–5, pp. 50–51	Act. 2, CD 2
¿Quién? vs. ¿Quiénes?	Act. 3, pp. 160–161	Act. 4, p. 38		
Talking about what you and your friends like to do together	Acts. 4–6, pp. 161–162	Act. 5, p. 39		
Vocabulario: Things you like to do with your friends	Acts. 4–6, pp. 161–162	Act. 6, p. 39		Act. 3, CD 2
The usage of the verb gustar	Act. 6, p. 162	Act. 7, p. 40		
-er and -ir verbs	Act. 5, p. 161	Acts. 8–10, pp. 40–41		Act. 4, CD 2
Talking about what you do during a typical week	Acts. 7, 8, pp. 162–163		Act. 12, p. 55	
Giving today's date	Act. 7, p. 162			
The formula for the date	Act. 7, p. 162	Acts. 12–14, pp. 42–43		
Vocabulario: The seasons	Act. 8, p. 163	Act. 11, p. 42	Acts. 13–15, p. 56	Act. 6, CD 2
Talking about the weather	Act. 9, p. 163			
Vocabulario: The weather	Act. 9, p. 163	Acts. 15–16, p. 44		Acts. 5, CD 2
CAPÍTULO 6	Más práctica gramatical	Cuaderno de gramática	Cuaderno de actividades	Interactive CD-ROM Tutor
Vocabulario: The family	Acts. 1, 2, p. 190	Acts. 1–2, p. 45	Act. 3, p. 62	Act. 1, CD 2
Describing a family	Act. 2, p. 190			
The possessive adjectives	Act. 1, 2, p. 190	Acts. 3–4, p. 46		Act. 2, CD 2
Describing people	Act. 2, p. 190			Act. 4, CD 2
Vocabulario: Adjectives	Act. 2, p. 190	Acts. 5–6, p. 47		
Discussing things a family does together	Act. 6, p. 192			
The verbs hacer and salir	Act. 3–5, p. 191	Acts. 8–9, pp. 48–49	Act. 13, p. 67	Act. 3, CD 2
The "personal a"	Act. 6, p. 192	Act. 10, p. 49	Act. 11, p. 66	
Discussing problems and giving advice	Act. 7–9, pp. 192–193			
The verb deber	Act. 7–8, pp. 192–193	Acts. 11–12, p. 50	Acts. 14–15, p. 68	
Vocabulario: Household chores	Act. 7, p. 192	Acts. 13–15, p. 51		Act. 5, CD 2
The verb poner	Act. 9, p. 193	Acts. 16–17, p. 52	Acts. 21–22, p. 69	Act. 6, CD 2

CAPÍTULO 7	Más práctica gramatical	Cuaderno de gramática	Cuaderno de actividades	Interactive CD-ROM Tutor
Talking on the phone		Acts. 1–2, p. 53	Acts. 3–4, p. 74	
Extending and accepting invitations				
e → ie stem-changing verbs	Act. 1–2, p. 222	Acts. 3–4, p. 54		Act. 2, CD 2
Vocabulario: Places	Act. 2–4, pp. 222–223	Acts. 5–7, p. 55		Act. 1, CD 2
Making plans	Act. 3, 4, p. 223			
The verb pensar and the structure ir + a + infinitive	Act. 5, p. 224	Acts. 8–11, pp. 56–57	Acts. 9–10, pp. 77–78	Act. 3, CD 2
Talking about getting ready	Act. 6, p. 224			Act. 4, CD 2
Reflexive verbs	Act. 6, p. 224	Acts. 12–13, p. 58		
Turning down an invitation and explaining why	Act. 7, p. 225	Acts. 14–15, p. 59		Act. 5, CD 2
Expressions with tener	Act. 8, p. 225	Acts. 16–17, p. 60	Acts. 15–17, pp. 81–82	Act. 6, CD 2
CAPÍTULO 8	Más práctica gramatical	Cuaderno de gramática	Cuaderno de actividades	Interactive CD-ROM Tutor
Talking about meals and food	Acts. 1, 3, pp. 252, 253			
Vocabulario: Meals	Acts. 1, 3, pp. 252, 253	Acts. 1–2, p. 61		
The verb encantar and indirect object pronouns	Act. 2, p. 252	Acts. 3–4, p. 62		
Vocabulario: Lunches	Act. 3, p. 253	Acts. 5–6, p. 63	Act. 7, p. 88	Act. 2, CD 2
o → ue stem-changing verbs	Act. 4, p. 253	Acts. 7–8, p. 64		Act. 1, CD 2
Commenting on food	Acts. 1–3, pp. 252–253			Act. 3, CD 2
ser vs. estar	Acts. 5–6, p. 254	Acts. 9–10, p. 65	Act. 11, p. 90	
More expressions with tener	Act. 7, pp. 254–255	Acts. 11–12, p. 66		
Making polite requests	Act. 8, p. 255			
Vocabulario: Utensils		Acts. 13–15, p. 67		
The forms of otro		Acts. 16–17, p. 68		
Vocabulario: Food	Act. 9, p. 255	Acts. 18–19, p. 69	Acts. 15–16, pp. 92–93	Act. 4, CD 2
Ordering dinner in a restaurant	Act. 8, p. 255			
Asking for and paying the bill in a restaurant				Act. 6, CD 2
Vocabulario: Numbers from 200 to 100, 000	Act. 9, p. 255	Acts. 20–21, p. 69		Act. 5, CD 2

Spanish 1 ¡Ven conmigo!

CAPÍTULO 9	Más práctica gramatical	Cuaderno de gramática	Cuaderno de actividades	Interactive CD-ROM Tutor
Discussing gift suggestions	Act. 1, p. 284		Act. 3, p. 98	Act. 2, CD 3
Vocabulario: Gift ideas	Act. 1–2, pp. 284–285	Acts. 1–2, p. 70		Act. 1, CD 3
Indirect Object Pronouns	Act. 2, p. 284	Acts. 3–5, pp. 71–72		
Asking for and giving directions downtown				
Vocabulario: Stores		Acts. 7–8, p. 73		
Commenting on clothes	Act. 3, p. 285			
Vocabulario: Clothes	Acts. 3–4, p. 285	Acts. 9–10, p. 74		Act. 4, CD 3
The usage of the preposition **de**	Act. 4, p. 285	Acts. 11–12, p. 75		
Vocabulario: More Clothes	Acts. 3–4, 6–8, pp. 285–287		Acts. 7–8, p. 101	
Así se dice Making comparisons	Act. 5, p. 286			
Gramática: Making comparisons	Act. 5, p. 286	Acts. 13–14, p. 76		Act. 3, CD 3
Expressing preferences	Acts. 6–7, pp. 286–287			
The demonstrative adjective **este**		Acts. 15–16, p. 77	Acts. 11–13, p. 104	Act. 6, CD 3
Asking about prices and paying for something	Act. 8, p. 287	Acts. 17–18, p. 78		Act. 5, CD 3
Vocabulario: Exclamatory expressions		Act. 19, p. 78		
CAPÍTULO 10	Más práctica gramatical	Cuaderno de gramática	Cuaderno de actividades	Interactive CD-ROM Tutor
Vocabulario: Holidays	Act. 1, p. 314	Act. 1, p. 79		Act. 1, CD 3
Talking about what you're doing right now	Acts. 2–3, pp. 314–315			
Present progressive	Acts. 2–3, pp. 314–315	Acts. 2–6, pp. 80–81		Act. 2, CD 3
Asking for and giving an opinion				
Asking for help and responding to requests	Acts. 4–5, pp. 315–316			
Vocabulario: Preparing for a party	Acts. 4–5, pp. 315–316	Acts. 7–8, p. 82		Act. 4, CD 3
Telling a friend what to do	Act. 5, p. 316			
Informal commands	Act. 5, p. 316	Acts. 9–12, pp. 83–84	Acts. 10–12, pp. 114–115	Act. 3, CD 3
Talking about past events	Acts. 6–7, pp. 316–317		Act. 22, p. 128	
Vocabulario: Talking about the past	Acts. 6–7, pp. 316–317	Acts. 16–17, p. 86		
The preterite of **-ar** verbs	Act. 6, p. 316	Acts. 13–15, pp. 85–86		Act. 5, CD 3
Direct object pronouns	Act. 8, p. 317	Acts. 18–21, pp. 87–88	Act. 16, p. 117	Act. 6, CD 3

CAPÍTULO 11	Más práctica gramatical	Cuaderno de gramática	Cuaderno de actividades	Interactive CD-ROM Tutor
Making suggestions and expressing feelings	Act. 1–2, p. 348		Act. 4, p. 122	
The verb **sentirse**	Act. 1–2, p. 348	Acts. 1–2, p. 89		Act. 1, CD 3
Vocabulario: Staying in shape	Act. 4, p. 349	Acts. 3–4, p. 90		Act. 2, CD 3
Talking about moods and physical condition	Act. 6, p. 350			
Vocabulario: Moods and health	Act. 6, p. 350	Acts. 5–7, pp. 91–92		Act. 3, CD 3
Vocabulario: Parts of the body	Act. 5, p. 359	Acts. 8–9, p. 92		Act. 4, CD 3
The verb **doler**	Act. 6. p. 350	Acts. 10–11, p. 93		
Saying what you did	Acts. 7–9, pp. 350–351			Act. 5, CD 3
The verb **jugar**	Acts. 7–8, p. 350–351	Acts. 12–13, p. 94		Act. 6, CD 3
Talking about where you went and when	Act. 8, p. 351			
The preterite of the verb **ir**	Act. 9, p. 351	Acts. 14–16, p. 95	Acts. 11–12, pp. 128–129	
Vocabulario: Places for sports	Act. 8, p. 351	Acts. 17–18, p. 96		

CAPÍTULO 12	Más práctica gramatical	Cuaderno de gramática	Cuaderno de actividades	Interactive CD-ROM Tutor
Talking about what you do and like to do every day	Acts. 1–3, p. 376			
Stem-changing verbs	Acts. 1–3, p. 376	Acts. 1–3, pp. 97–98		Act. 2, CD 3
Making future plans	Act. 5, p. 377			
Vocabulario: Clothes to take on vacation		Acts. 4–7, pp. 99–100	Act. 6, p. 136	Act. 1, CD 3
Verbs + infinitives	Act. 5, p. 377	Acts. 8–10, pp. 101–102		
Vocabulario: Things to do on vacation	Acts. 6–8, p. 378	Act. 12, p. 103		Act. 3, CD 3
Discussing what you would like to do on vacation	Acts. 6–8, p. 378			
ser and **estar**	Acts. 7–8, p. 378	Acts. 13–16, pp. 104–105		Act. 4, CD 3
Saying where you went and what you did on vacation	Act. 9, p. 379		Acts. 15–16, pp. 141–142	Act. 5, CD 3
Preterite tense	Act. 9, p. 379	Acts. 17–18, p. 106		Act. 6, CD 3
Vocabulario: Foreign countries	Act. 9, p. 379	Acts. 19–20, p. 107		

Spanish 1 ¡Ven conmigo!

Student Make-Up Assignments Checklist

P Capítulo preliminar

■ CAPITULO PRELIMINAR Student Make-Up Assignments Checklist

Pupil's Edition, pp. 1–11

The material on pages 5–9 can best be learned and practiced in conjunction with Audio CD 1 in the Audio Program.

Study the map of Spanish-speaking countries on pages xxx–1	☐ Find the countries where the Spanish speakers pictured on the map live.
Read page 2: El español—¿Por qué?	☐ Write five reasons for learning Spanish. Which of the reasons is most important to you?
Read the information on page 3.	☐ Read the five questions on page 3 (Herencia hispana) and choose one as a written assignment.
Read the information on p. 4.	☐ List other native Spanish-speakers of whom you are aware, along with some of their accomplishments.
Study nombres comunes on page 5.	☐ Do Activity 3, p. 5.
Study el alfabeto on pages 6–7.	☐ Do Activity 5, p. 6 as a writing activity. ☐ Do Activity 6, p. 7 as a writing activity. ☐ Do Activity 7, p. 7 as a writing activity.
Study the frases útiles on page 8.	☐ Do Activity 9, p. 8 as a writing activity.
Study the colores y números on page 9.	☐ Do Activity 10, p. 9 as a writing activity. ☐ Do Activity 12, p. 9 as a writing activity. ☐ Do Activity 14, p. 10 as a writing activity.
Read the information on page 11: Sugerencias para aprender el español.	☐ Be prepared to discuss the tips for learning Spanish with the class.

Spanish 1 ¡Ven conmigo!

Nombre _____ Clase _____ Fecha _____

¡Mucho Gusto!

■ PRIMER PASO Student Make-Up Assignments Checklist
Pupil's Edition, pp. 21–25

Study the expressions in the **Así se dice** box on page 21: saying hello and goodbye. You should know how to greet someone and how to say goodbye to someone.	☐ Activity 7, p. 22. Write how you would say hello to the people in the pictures and how they would respond.
	☐ Activity 8, p. 22. Write the conversation between you and a friend if you ran into each other in the hall between classes. Greet each other briefly, tell your partner you have to go, and say goodbye.
	☐ For additional practice, do Activity 1, p. 1. in the **Cuaderno de gramática**.
Study the expressions in the **Así se dice** box on page 22: introducing people and responding to an introduction. You should know how to introduce yourself, how to respond to an introduction, and how to introduce others.	☐ Do Activity 10, p. 23. Write what you would say in those situations. Find the expressions you need in **Así se dice**.
	☐ Do Activity 11, p. 23. Complete the conversation. Use expressions you've learned.
	☐ For additional practice, do Activity 2, p. 38 in **Más práctica gramatical**.
	☐ For additional practice, do Activity 2, p. 1 in the **Cuaderno de gramática**.
Study the grammar presentation in the **Nota gramatical** box on page 23: diacritical signs	☐ Do Activity 12, p. 24. Write out the conversation with expressions from **Así se dice**.
	☐ For additional practice, do Activity 1, p. 38 in **Más práctica gramatical**.
	☐ For additional practice, do Activity 3–5, p. 2 in the **Cuaderno de gramática**.
Study the expressions in the **Así se dice** box on page 24: asking how someone is and saying how you are. You should know how to find out how a friend is and how to say how you are.	☐ Do Activity 14, p. 24. Write how you would answer the statements in the activity. Select your responses from the expressions you've learned.
	☐ For additional practice, do Activity 2, p. 38 in **Más práctica gramatical**.
	☐ For additional practice, do Activities 5–7, pp. 5–6 in the **Cuaderno de actividades**.

☐ For additional practice, do Activities 6–7, p. 3 in the **Cuaderno de gramática.**

☐ For additional practice, do Activities 1–2, CD 1 in the **Interactive CD-ROM Tutor.**

Study the grammar presentation in the **Gramática** box on page 25: subject pronouns **tú** and **you.** You should know how and when to use the personal pronouns.

☐ Do Activity 16, p. 25. Write the conversation that Mercedes is having, using words or phrases you've learned.

☐ Do Activity 17, p. 25. Write another conversation among three friends in which one person is being introduced to another.

☐ For additional practice, do Activity 3, p. 38 in **Más práctica gramatical.**

☐ For additional practice, do Activities 8–10, p. 4 in the **Cuaderno de gramática.**

■ PRIMER PASO Self-Test

Can you say hello and goodbye?	How would you greet or say goodbye to these people?
	1. your best friend
	2. the principal before classes
	3. a classmate as the bell rings
	4. your neighbor as he or she leaves your house one evening
	5. a friend at the end of a school day
Can you introduce people and respond to an introduction?	What would you say in the following situations?
	1. You want to introduce yourself to an interesting new classmate at a party.
	2. The new Spanish teacher asks your name.
	3. You have just been introduced to Juan, the new exchange student from Spain.
	4. Juan has just said, "Mucho gusto."
Can you ask how someone is and say how you are?	Juan has just joined your class and you want to get to know him. How would you . . . ?
	1. ask him how he is doing
	2. tell him how you're doing

For an **online self-test**, go to **go.hrw.com.**

WV3 SPAIN–1

Nombre _____ Clase _____ Fecha _____

¡Mucho Gusto!

■ SEGUNDO PASO Student Make-Up Assignments Checklist

Pupil's Edition, pp. 27–30

Study the expressions in the **Así se dice** box on page 27: asking and saying how old someone is. You should know how to ask how old someone is and say how old you are.	☐ Do Activity 20, p. 28. Write a conversation between three classmates in which they introduce themselves to each other, greet each other, and ask each other's names and ages. ☐ For additional practice, do Activity 7, p. 41 in **Más práctica gramatical**.
Study the **Vocabulario** on page 27.	☐ For additional practice, do Activities 11–13, p. 5 in the **Cuaderno de gramática**. ☐ For additional practice, do Activity 3, CD 1 in the **Interactive CD-ROM Tutor**.
Study the expressions in the **Así se dice** box on page 28: asking where someone is from and saying where you're from. You should know how to find out where someone is from and say where you are from.	☐ For additional practice, do Activity 6, p. 40 in **Más práctica gramatical**. ☐ For additional practice, do Activities 11–13, p. 8 in the **Cuaderno de actividades**.
Study the grammar presentation in the **Nota gramatical** box on page 28: forms of the verb **ser**.	☐ Do Activity 23, p. 29. Make a list of five famous women and five famous men. Include as many Spanish speakers as you can. Then, next to each person's name, write where he or she is from. ☐ Do Activity 24, p. 29. ☐ For additional practice, do Activity 5, p. 39 in **Más práctica gramatical**. ☐ For additional practice, do Activity 14, p. 6 in the **Cuaderno de gramática**.
Study the grammar presentation in the **Gramática** box on page 30: forming questions with question words. You should know how to use and identify question words.	☐ Do Activity 25, p. 30. ☐ Do Activity 26, p. 30. ☐ Do Activity 28, p. 30. Write a brief paragraph telling the name of your best friend, how he or she is, and where he or she is from.

☐ For additional practice, do Activity 7, p. 41 in **Más práctica gramatical.**

☐ For additional practice, do Activity 15, p. 6 in the **Cuaderno de gramática.**

☐ For additional practice, do Activity 4, CD 1 in the **Interactive CD-ROM Tutor.**

■ SEGUNDO PASO Self-Test

Can you ask and say how old someone is?	How would you . . . ?
	1. ask Juan, the new exchange student from Spain, how old he is
	2. tell him how old you are
	3. tell your friend how old Juan is
Can you ask where someone is from, and say where you're from?	Can you . . . ?
	1. tell Juan where you're from
	2. tell the new Spanish teacher your name
	3. ask him where he is from
	4. tell your friend where Juan is from

 For an **online self-test**, go to **go.hrw.com.**

WV3 SPAIN–1

CAPÍTULO 1 ¡Mucho Gusto!

■ TERCER PASO Student Make-Up Assignments Checklist

Pupil's Edition, pp. 32–35

Study the expressions in the **Así se dice** box on page 32: talking about likes and dislikes. You should know how to find out what a friend likes and how to say what you like and do not like.	☐ For additional practice, do Activities 8–9, p. 41 in **Más práctica gramatical**.
Study the **Vocabulario** on page 32.	☐ For additional practice, do Activities 16–17, p. 7 in the **Cuaderno de gramática**. ☐ For additional practice, do Activity 6, CD 1 in the **Interactive CD-ROM Tutor**.
Study the grammar presentation in the **Gramática** box on page 33: nouns and definite articles. You should know how to use the definite articles.	☐ Do Activity 30, p. 33. ☐ Do Activity 31, p. 33. Write questions asking a classmate whether he or she likes the sports, music, food, and schoolwork listed in the **Vocabulario** on page 32. ☐ Do Activity 34, p. 34. ☐ Do Activity 37, p. 35. ☐ For additional practice, do Activity 9, p. 41 in **Más práctica gramatical**. ☐ For additional practice, do Activities 18–20, p. 8 in the **Cuaderno de gramática**.

CAPÍTULO 1

■ TERCER PASO Self-Test

Can you talk about likes and dislikes?	You'd like to ask Juan, the new exchange student from Spain, to do something with you on Saturday, but you don't know what he likes. Ask him if he likes these things, and tell him which ones you like.

1. Chinese food

2. rock music

3. volleyball

4. baseball

5. Italian food

6. pop music

7. swimming

8. basketball

9. jazz

 For an **online self-test**, go to **go.hrw.com**.

WV3 SPAIN–1

¡Organízate!

■ PRIMER PASO Student Make-Up Assignments Checklist

Pupil's Edition, pp. 51–54

Study the **Vocabulario** on page 51.	☐ For additional practice, do Activity 3, p. 14 in the **Cuaderno de actividades**. ☐ For additional practice, do Activities 1–2, p. 9 in the **Cuaderno de gramática**. ☐ For additional practice, do Activity 1, CD 1 in the **Interactive CD-ROM Tutor**.
Study the grammar presentation in the **Nota gramatical** box on page 51: indefinite articles.	☐ Do Activity 7, p. 51. ☐ For additional practice, do Activities 1, 3, p. 66 in **Más práctica gramatical**. ☐ For additional practice, do Activities 3–4, p. 10 in the **Cuaderno de actividades**.
Study the expressions in the **Así se dice** box on page 52: talking about what you want and need. You should know how to find out what someone wants and needs, and say what you want and need.	☐ Do Activity 9, p. 48. ☐ For additional practice, do Activity 5, p. 67 in **Más práctica gramatical**.
Study the grammar presentation in the **Gramática** box on page 52: making nouns plural. You should know how to make the plural forms of nouns.	☐ Do Activity 10, p. 49. Write the conversation between Paco and a friend. Each time Paco says he wants an item, his friend tells him he already has several. Follow the model. ☐ Do Activity 11, p. 49. Write sentences saying what you have and what you need, using the images on the page. ☐ Do Activity 12, p. 49. Write a paragraph using the sentences you wrote for Activity 11. ☐ For additional practice, do Activities 5–6, p. 11 in the **Cuaderno de gramática**.

Study the grammar presentation in the **Gramática** box on page 53: indefinite articles. You should know how to use indefinite articles.	☐ Do Activity 13, p. 54. ☐ Do Activity 14, p. 54. ☐ For additional practice, do Activities 1, 3, p. 66 in **Más práctica gramatical**. ☐ For additional practice, do Activities 7–8, p. 12 in the **Cuaderno de gramática**. ☐ For additional practice, do Activity 2, CD 1 in the **Interactive CD-ROM Tutor**.
Study the grammar presentation in the **Nota gramatical** box on page 54: subject pronouns **él** and **ella**.	☐ Do Activity 15, p. 50. ☐ For additional practice, do Activities 4, 5, p. 67 in **Más práctica gramatical**. ☐ For additional practice, do Activities 9–10, p. 13 in the **Cuaderno de gramática**.

■ PRIMER PASO Self-Test

| Can you talk about what you want and need? | How would you ask these students if they need the items listed? How would the students answer?

1. Juanita   some pens and paper
2. Paco   a calculator
3. Felipe   some notebooks
4. Mercedes   a backpack
5. Tú   ¿? |

For an **online self-test**, go to **go.hrw.com**.

WV3 SPAIN–2

Spanish 1 ¡Ven conmigo!, Chapter 2

¡Organízate!

■ SEGUNDO PASO Student Make-Up Assignments Checklist

Pupil's Edition, pp. 56–59

Study the **Vocabulario** on page 56.	☐ Do Activity 17, p. 56. ☐ For additional practice, do Activities 11–12, p. 14 in the **Cuaderno de gramática**. ☐ For additional practice, do Activity 3, CD 1 in the **Interactive CD-ROM Tutor**.
Study the expressions in the **Así se dice** box on page 57: describing the contents of your room. You should know how to find out what there is in someone's room and how to say what is in your room.	☐ Do Activity 18, p. 57. ☐ Do Activity 19, p. 57. ☐ Do Activity 20, p. 57. Look at the art on page 56, and then write what there is in your room. ☐ For additional practice, do Activity 6, p. 67 in **Más práctica gramatical**.
Study the grammar presentation in the **Gramática** box on page 58: agreement of **mucho** and **¿cuánto?** with nouns.	☐ Do Activity 21, p. 54. ☐ Do Activity 22, p. 55. Write a comparison of the rooms in the pictures by describing what there is or is not in them. ☐ Do Activity 23, p. 55. Write a description of what there is in the ideal classroom. ☐ Do Activity 24, p. 55. ☐ For additional practice, do Activity 7, p. 68 in **Más práctica gramatical**. ☐ For additional practice, do Activities 11–13, pp. 18–19 in the **Cuaderno de actividades**. ☐ For additional practice, do Activity 13, pp. 15 in the **Cuaderno de actividades**. ☐ For additional practice, do Activity 4, CD 1 in the **Interactive CD-ROM Tutor**.

■ SEGUNDO PASO Self-Test

Can you describe the contents of your room?	How would you tell a friend how many, if any, of each item is in your room? How would you say you don't have a certain item but want one? Now write out the questions you would use to ask your friend if she or he has these items in his or her room?

1. a closet
2. a bed
3. a radio
4. a TV set

Tomorrow is the first day of class. Ask a friend how much or how many he or she needs of these things. How would your friend answer?

1. paper
2. books
3. rulers
4. notebooks
5. folders
6. pencils

 For an **online self-test**, go to **go.hrw.com**.

WV3 SPAIN–2

CAPÍTULO 2

CAPÍTULO

2 ¡Organízate!

■ TERCER PASO Student Make-Up Assignments Checklist

Pupil's Edition, pp. 60–63

Study the expressions in the **Así se dice** box on page 60: talking about what you need and want to do. You should know how to find out what someone needs and wants to do and how to say what you need and want to do.	☐ Do Activity 25, p. 60. ☐ Do Activity 26, p. 60. Write a conversation between two people similar to the ones in Activity 25. Be creative. ☐ For additional practice, do Activities 8–9, pp. 68–69 in **Más práctica gramatical**. ☐ For additional practice, do Activities 14–17, pp. 20–21in the **Cuaderno de actividades**. ☐ For additional practice, do Activity 5, CD 1 in the **Interactive CD-ROM Tutor**.
Study the **Vocabulario** on page 61.	☐ For additional practice, do Activity 9, p. 69 in **Más práctica gramatical**. ☐ For additional practice, do Activity 14, p. 16 in the **Cuaderno de gramática**.
Study the grammar presentation in the **Nota gramatical** box on page 61: the verbs **comprar, poner, conocer,** and **ir** (the infinitive forms).	☐ Do Activity 28, p. 61 as a writing activity. ☐ Do Activity 29, p. 61. ☐ Do Activity 31, p. 62. Write a conversation in which two friends who are going back to school tell each other what they need to buy and how much money they need. ☐ For additional practice, do Activity 15, p. 16 in the **Cuaderno de gramática**.
Study the **Vocabulario** on page 62.	☐ Do Activity 32, p. 62 as a writing activity. ☐ Do Activity 33, p. 63 as a writing activity. ☐ Do Activity 35, p. 63 as a writing activity. ☐ For additional practice, do Activities 16–17, p. 17 in the **Cuaderno de gramática**. ☐ For additional practice, do Activity 6, CD 1 in the **Interactive CD-ROM Tutor**.

CAPÍTULO 2

■ TERCER PASO Self-Test

Can you talk about what you need and want to do?	How would you say you need to do the following things? How would you say you want to do the same things? 1. to organize your room 2. to put your tennis shoes in the closet 3. to find your money 4. to go to the bookstore 5. to buy a lot of things 6. to meet some new friends

 For an **online self-test**, go to **go.hrw.com**.

WV3 SPAIN–2

CAPÍTULO 2

CAPÍTULO

3 Nuevas clases, nuevos amigos

■ PRIMER PASO Student Make-Up Assignments Checklist

Pupil's Edition, pp. 83–86

Study the **Vocabulario** on page 83.	☐ For additional practice, do Activities 1–2, p. 18 in the **Cuaderno de gramática**. ☐ For additional practice, do Activity 3, CD 1 in the **Interactive CD-ROM Tutor**.
Study the grammar presentation in the **Nota gramatical** box on page 83: the plural forms of the definite articles.	☐ For additional practice, do Activity 1, p. 100 in **Más práctica gramatical**. ☐ For additional practice, do Activities 3–5, p. 19 in the **Cuaderno de gramática**.
Study the expressions in the **Así se dice** box on page 84: talking about classes and sequencing events. You should know how to find out what classes a friend has and how to say what classes you have.	☐ Do Activity 7, p. 84. Write your answers. ☐ Do Activity 8, p. 84. ☐ Do Activity 9, p. 85. Write a conversation between two friends. They should greet each other, each ask how the other is, and find out what classes the other has. Use expressions you've learned for talking about your schedule. ☐ For additional practice, do Activities 2, 4, p. 100–101 in **Más práctica gramatical**.
Study the expressions in the **Así se dice** box on page 85: telling time. You should know how to find out what time it is and how to say what time it is.	☐ For additional practice, do Activities 2–3, p. 100–101 in **Más práctica gramatical**. ☐ For additional practice, do Activity 1, CD 1 in the **Interactive CD-ROM Tutor**.
Study the grammar presentation in the **Gramática** box on page 86: telling time.	☐ Do Activity 11, p. 85 ☐ Do Activity 12, p. 86. Write the time that each of the watches displays. ☐ Do Activity 14, p. 86. ☐ For additional practice, do Activities 2–3, pp. 100–101 in **Más práctica gramatical**. ☐ For additional practice, do Activities 7–8, p. 28 in the **Cuaderno de actividades**. ☐ For additional practice, do Activities 6–7, p. 20 in the **Cuaderno de gramática**. ☐ For additional practice, do Activity 2, CD 1 in the **Interactive CD-ROM Tutor**.

CAPÍTULO 3

■ PRIMER PASO Self-Test

Can you talk about classes and sequence events?	How would you tell a classmate the sequence of your classes today? and tomorrow?
Can you tell time?	Write out these times. 1. 5:46 2. 8:30 3. 7:50 4. 10:10

 For an **online self-test**, go to **go.hrw.com**.

WV3 Mexico–3

CAPÍTULO 3

Nuevas clases, nuevos amigos

■ SEGUNDO PASO Student Make-Up Assignments Checklist

Pupil's Edition, pp. 88–90

Study the expressions in the **Así se dice** box on page 88: telling at what time something happens. You should know how to find out at what time something happens and say when something happens.	☐ Do Activity 16, p. 88. Write when these classes meet. Use the time listed for each course. ☐ Do Activity 17, p. 89. Select a show in each time slot you want to watch, and write a sentence. ☐ For additional practice, do Activities 3–4, p. 100 in **Más práctica gramatical**.
Study the **Vocabulario** on page 88.	☐ For additional practice, do Activity 3, p. 101 in **Más práctica gramatical**. ☐ For additional practice, do Activities 8–9, p. 21 in the **Cuaderno de gramática**.
Study the grammar presentation in the **Nota gramatical** box on page 89: using **de** to express possession.	☐ Do Activity 19, p. 89. Complete the sentences in writing. ☐ For additional practice, do Activity 5, p. 102 in **Más práctica gramatical**. ☐ For additional practice, do Activities 10–11, p. 22 in the **Cuaderno de gramática**.
Study the expressions in the **Así se dice** box on page 90: talking about being late or in a hurry. You should know how to say that you are late or in a hurry and that someone else is late or in a hurry.	☐ Do Activity 20, p. 90. ☐ Do Activity 21, p. 90. ☐ Do Activity 22, p. 90. ☐ For additional practice, do Activities 11–12, pp. 30–31 in the **Cuaderno de actividades**. ☐ For additional practice, do Activity 4, CD 1 in the **Interactive CD-ROM Tutor**.

CAPÍTULO 3

■ SEGUNDO PASO Self-Test

Can you tell at what time something happens?	How would you ask each of these students what classes they have and at what time the classes meet? How would each student answer?

1. Sofía—physical education (8:13)
   —art (2:10)

2. César—French (11:40)
   —geography (2:25)

3. Simón—social sciences (9:07)
   —mathematics (3:15)

4. Adela—science (10:38)
   —computer science (12:54)

Can you talk about being late or in a hurry?	How would you . . . ?

1. say that you are in a hurry

2. say that you are late

3. say that a friend is late

4. tell a friend to hurry up

 For an **online self-test**, go to **go.hrw.com**.

WV3 Mexico–3

CAPÍTULO 3

CAPÍTULO 3

Nuevas clases, nuevos amigos

■ TERCER PASO Student Make-Up Assignments Checklist

Pupil's Edition, pp. 92–97

Study the expressions in the **Así se dice** box on page 92: describing people and things. You should know how to find out what people and things are like and how to say what someone or something is like.	☐ For additional practice, do Activities 6–7, pp. 102–103 in **Más práctica gramatical**.
Study the grammar presentation in the **Nota gramatical** box on page 92: the plural forms of **ser**.	☐ Do Activity 23, p. 92. Write each of the sentences and your answer. ☐ For additional practice, do Activity 7, p. 103 in **Más práctica gramatical**. ☐ For additional practice, do Activities 12–13, p. 123 in the **Cuaderno de gramática**.
Study the **Vocabulario** on page 92.	☐ For additional practice, do Activities 6–8, pp. 102–103 in **Más práctica gramatical**. ☐ For additional practice, do Activities 14–15, p. 24 in the **Cuaderno de gramática**. ☐ For additional practice, do Activity 6, CD 1 in the **Interactive CD-ROM Tutor**.
Study the grammar presentation in the **Gramática** box on page 93: adjective agreement.	☐ Do Activity 24, p. 93. ☐ Do Activity 25, p. 94 as a writing activity. ☐ Do Activity 26, p. 94 as a writing activity. ☐ Do Activity 27, p. 94 as a writing activity. ☐ Do Activity 28, p. 94 ☐ For additional practice, do Activity 7, p. 103 in **Más práctica gramatical**. ☐ For additional practice, do Activities 16–17, pp. 33–34 in the **Cuaderno de actividades**. ☐ For additional practice, do Activity 17, p. 25 in the **Cuaderno de gramática**.
Study the expressions in the **Así se dice** box on page 95: talking about things you like and explaining why. You should know how to find out if a friend likes more than one thing and how to say you like more than one thing.	☐ Do Activity 30, p. 96 as a writing activity. ☐ For additional practice, do Activity 8, p. 103 in **Más práctica gramatical**.

CAPÍTULO 3

Spanish 1 ¡Ven conmigo!, Chapter 3

Student Make-Up Assignments **19**

Study the **Vocabulario** on page 95.	☐ Do Activity 30, p. 96 as a writing activity.
	☐ For additional practice, do Activity 8, p. 103 in **Más práctica gramatical**.
	☐ For additional practice, do Activities 18–19, p. 26 in the **Cuaderno de gramática**.
Study the grammar presentation in the **Nota gramatical** box on page 96: tag questions.	☐ Do Activity 31, p. 96. Write a conversation between two friends in which they ask each other whether they like the shows in the entertainment guide. Use tag questions.
	☐ Do Activity 32, p. 96. Write questions you can use to interview a student. Ask about age, classes, friends, teachers, likes, and dislikes.
	☐ Do Activity 34, p. 97. Write a detailed description of your best friend. Include the person's age, personality traits, physical characteristics, and the person's likes and dislikes.
	☐ Do Activity 35, p. 97.
	☐ For additional practice, do Activity 14, p. 32 in the **Cuaderno de actividades**.

■ TERCER PASO Self-Test

Can you describe people and things?	Imagine you're an exchange student in Cuernavaca. Describe the following people and things in your school in the U.S. to your new friends in Cuernavaca.
	1. the teachers
	2. Spanish class
	3. the exams
	4. physical education class
	5. school friends
	6. art class
Can you talk about things you like and explain why?	How would you say which activities and classes you like or dislike, and why? How would you ask a friend for the same information? How would you report what your friend likes and doesn't like?

 For an **online self-test**, go to **go.hrw.com**.

WV3 Mexico–3

CAPÍTULO 3

CAPÍTULO 4

¿Qué haces esta tarde?

■ PRIMER PASO Student Make-Up Assignments Checklist

Pupil's Edition, pp. 113–117

Study the expressions in the **Así se dice** box on page 113: talking about what you like to do. You should know how to find out what a friend likes to do and how to say what you like to do.	☐ Do the first part of Activity 7, p. 113. ☐ For additional practice, do Activity 3, p. 38 in the **Cuaderno de actividades.** ☐ For additional practice, do Activities 1–2, p. 27 in the **Cuaderno de gramática.**
Study the **Vocabulario** on page 113.	☐ For additional practice, do Activities 1–3, pp. 128–129 in **Más práctica gramatical.** ☐ For additional practice, do Activity 1, CD 1 in the **Interactive CD-ROM Tutor.**
Study the grammar presentation in the **Gramática** box on page 114: present tense of regular –ar verbs.	☐ For additional practice, do Activity 1, p. 128 in **Más práctica gramatical.** ☐ For additional practice, do Activities 3–4, p. 28 in the **Cuaderno de gramática.** ☐ For additional practice, do Activity 2, CD 1 in the **Interactive CD–ROM Tutor.**
Study the expressions in the **Así se dice** box on page 114: discussing what you and others do during free time. You should know how to ask a friend what he or she likes to do after school and how to say what you like to do after school.	☐ Do Activity 9, p. 115. ☐ Do Activity 10, p. 116. ☐ Do Activity 11, p. 116. ☐ For additional practice, do Activities 1-3, pp. 128–129 in **Más práctica gramatical.** ☐ For additional practice, do Activities 5–6, p. 29 in the **Cuaderno de gramática.**
Study the **Vocabulario** on page 115.	☐ Do Activity 9, p. 115.

CAPÍTULO 4

Study the grammar presentation in the **Nota gramatical** box on page 116: the preposition **con**.

☐ Do the part of Activity 13, p. 116, that pertains to you. Write who does the activities with you.

☐ Do Activity 15, p. 117.

☐ For additional practice, do Activity 2, p. 128 in **Más práctica gramatical**.

☐ For additional practice, do Activity 8, p. 30 in the **Cuaderno de gramática**.

Study the grammar presentation in the **Nota gramatical** box on page 117: **que**.

☐ Do Activity 16, p. 116 as a writing activity; write about yourself.

☐ For additional practice, do Activity 3, p. 129 in **Más práctica gramatical**.

☐ For additional practice, do Activity 9, p. 30 in the **Cuaderno de gramática**.

■ PRIMER PASO Self-Test

Can you talk about what you like to do?

Write a sentence telling what these people like to do at the place given.

MODELO   Mr. López - la oficina
               Le gusta trabajar.

1. Cecilia - la piscina

2. Gustavo - el centro comercial

3. Diego y Berta - la fiesta

4. Carlos y yo - el parque

5. Linda y Eva - la biblioteca

6. yo - el colegio

Can you discuss what you and others do during free time?

How would you tell someone that you . . . ?

1. play the guitar

2. wash the car

3. prepare dinner

4. paint and draw

5. watch television

6. swim in the pool

For an **online self-test**, go to **go.hrw.com**.

WV3 Mexico–4

Nombre _____ Clase _____ Fecha _____

4 ¿Qué haces esta tarde?

■ SEGUNDO PASO Student Make-Up Assignments Checklist

Pupil's Edition, pp. 118–121

Study the expressions in the **Así se dice** box on page 118: telling where people and things are. You should know how to find out where someone or something is, and how to say where someone or something is and where you are.	☐ For additional practice, do Activities 4–5, p. 129 in **Más práctica gramatical.** ☐ For additional practice, do Activity 3, CD 1 in the **Interactive CD-ROM Tutor.**
Study the grammar presentation in the **Nota gramatical** box on page 118: the verb **estar.**	☐ Do Activity 19, p. 118. ☐ Do Activity 20, p. 119 as a writing activity. ☐ For additional practice, do Activities 4–6, pp. 129–130 in **Más práctica gramatical.** ☐ For additional practice, do Activities 10–11, p. 31 in the **Cuaderno de gramática.** ☐ For additional practice, do Activity 4, CD 1 in the **Interactive CD-ROM Tutor.**
Study the **Vocabulario** on page 119.	☐ Do Activity 22, p. 120 as a writing activity. ☐ Do Activity 24, p. 121 as a writing activity. ☐ For additional practice, do Activities 8–9, pp. 41–42 in the **Cuaderno de actividades.** ☐ For additional practice, do Activities 12–13, p. 32 in the **Cuaderno de gramática.**
Study the grammar presentation in the **Gramática** box on page 121: subject pronouns.	☐ Do Activity 25, p. 121. ☐ For additional practice, do Activities 5–7, pp. 129–130 in **Más práctica gramatical.** ☐ For additional practice, do Activities 14–16, p. 33 in the **Cuaderno de gramática.**

Spanish 1 ¡Ven conmigo!, Chapter 4

Student Make-Up Assignments **23**

■ SEGUNDO PASO Self-Test

Can you tell where people and things are?

Write sentences in Spanish telling where the following people are.

1. Rosa is reading books and must be very quiet.
2. Claudia is shopping for gifts for her parents.
3. Gerardo is walking the dogs.
4. Sofía is exercising and lifting weights.
5. You and your friends are watching a movie.
6. You're talking on the phone.

How would you tell a visitor who needs directions that . . . ?

1. the supermarket is next to the park
2. the bookstore is far from the store
3. the gym is near the library

For an **online self-test**, go to **go.hrw.com**.

WV3 Mexico–4

CAPÍTULO

4 ¿Qué haces esta tarde?

■ **TERCER PASO** Student Make-Up Assignments Checklist

Pupil's Edition, pp. 123–125

Study the expressions in the **Así se dice** box on page 123: talking about where you and others go during free time. You should know how to find out where someone is going and how to say where you are going.	☐ For additional practice, do Activities 7-9, pp. 130–131 in **Más práctica gramatical.**
Study the grammar presentation in the **Nota gramatical** box on page 123: the verb **ir.**	☐ Do Activity 27, p. 123. ☐ Do Activity 28, p. 124 as a writing activity. ☐ Do Activity 29, p. 124. ☐ For additional practice, do Activity 7 p. 130 in **Más práctica gramatical.** ☐ For additional practice, do Activities 11–12, p. 44 in the **Cuaderno de actividades.** ☐ For additional practice, do Activities 17–18, p. 37 in the **Cuaderno de gramática.** ☐ For additional practice, do Activity 5, CD 1 in the **Interactive CD-ROM Tutor.**
Study the **Vocabulario** on page 124.	☐ For additional practice, do Activities 8–9, p. 131 in **Más práctica gramatical.** ☐ For additional practice, do Activities 19–20, p. 35 in the **Cuaderno de gramática.** ☐ For additional practice, do Activity 6, CD 1 in the **Interactive CD-ROM Tutor.**
Study the grammar presentation in the **Nota gramatical** box on page 124: the days of the week.	☐ Do Activity 30, p. 125 as a writing activity. Refer to your schedule to answer. ☐ Do Activity 32, p. 125. ☐ For additional practice, do Activity 8, p. 131 in **Más práctica gramatical.** ☐ For additional practice, do Activities 21–23, p. 36 in the **Cuaderno de gramática.**

CAPÍTULO 4

■ TERCER PASO Self-Test

| Can you talk about where you and others go during free time? | Create a sentence telling where each person is going and why. |

Create a sentence telling where each person is going and why.

MODELO Mr. Suárez is really thirsty.
            Él va al restaurante para tomar un refresco.

1. Mariana wants to buy some books, notebooks, and pencils.

2. Pedro needs to talk to his English teacher.

3. Lupe wants to spend time with her friend.

4. Mrs. Suárez and her sister want to go swimming.

5. Carlos and Adriana need to buy stamps.

6. You and a friend want to play tennis.

Think of a typical week in your life. Write a sentence telling at what time and on which day you're at the following places.

1. el centro comercial

2. el cine

3. la casa de un amigo/una amiga

4. el parque

For an **online self-test**, go to **go.hrw.com**.

WV3 Mexico–4

CAPÍTULO

5 El ritmo de la vida

■ **PRIMER PASO** Student Make-Up Assignments Checklist

Pupil's Edition, pp. 145–147

Study the expressions in the **Así se dice** box on page 145: discussing how often you do things. You should know how to find out how often a friend does things and how to say how often you do things.	☐ For additional practice, do Activities 1, 2, p. 160 in **Más práctica gramatical.** ☐ For additional practice, do Activity 1, CD 2 in the **Interactive CD-ROM Tutor.**
Study the grammar presentation in the **Gramática** box on page 145: negation.	☐ Do Activity 7, p. 146 as a writing activity. ☐ Do Activity 8, p. 146. ☐ Do Activity 9, p. 146 as a writing activity. Write about yourself. ☐ For additional practice, do Activity 2, p. 160 in **Más práctica gramatical.** ☐ For additional practice, do Activities 3–5, pp. 50–51 in the **Cuaderno de actividades.** ☐ For additional practice, do Activities 1–3, pp. 37–38 in the **Cuaderno de gramática.** ☐ For additional practice, do Activity 2, CD 2 in the **Interactive CD-ROM Tutor.**
Study the grammar presentation in the **Nota gramatical** box on page 146: the plural of **¿quién?**	☐ Do Activity 10, p. 146. ☐ Do Activity 11, p. 147 as a writing activity. ☐ For additional practice, do Activity 3, pp. 160–161 in **Más práctica gramatical.** ☐ For additional practice, do Activity 4, p. 38 in the **Cuaderno de gramática.**

CAPÍTULO 5

■ **PRIMER PASO** Self-Test

Can you discuss how often you do things?	How would José Luis say that . . . ?
	1. he never swims
	2. he always eats breakfast
	3. he sometimes talks to Luisa
	4. he always works on the weekends
	5. he sometimes goes to the movies on Fridays
	6. he never studies in the library
	7. he always helps at home

 For an **online self-test**, go to **go.hrw.com**.

WV3 FLORIDA–5

CAPÍTULO 6

5 El ritmo de la vida

■ SEGUNDO PASO Student Make-Up Assignments Checklist

Pupil's Edition, pp. 148–152

Study the expressions in the **Así se dice** box on page 148: telling about what you and your friends like to do together. You should know how to find out what some of your friends like to do and how to say what you and friends like to do and what your friends like to do.	☐ Do Activity 14, p. 149 as a writing activity. ☐ For additional practice, do Activities 4–9, pp. 161–162 in **Más práctica gramatical.** ☐ For additional practice, do Activity 5, p. 39 in the **Cuaderno de gramática.**
Study the **Vocabulario** on page 149.	☐ For additional practice, do Activity 6, p. 39 in the **Cuaderno de gramática.** ☐ For additional practice, do Activity 3, CD 2 in the **Interactive CD-ROM Tutor.**
Study the grammar presentation in the **Nota gramatical** box on page 149: the usage of the verb **gustar.**	☐ Do Activity 15, p. 149 as a writing activity. Write about yourself. ☐ For additional practice, do Activity 6, p. 162 in **Más práctica gramatical.** ☐ For additional practice, do Activities 7, p. 40 in the **Cuaderno de gramática.**
Study the grammar presentation in the **Gramática** box on page 150: -**er** and -**ir** verbs.	☐ Do Activity 16, p. 150. ☐ Do Activity 17, p. 151 as a writing activity. ☐ For additional practice, do Activity 5, p. 161 in **Más práctica gramatical.** ☐ For additional practice, do Activities 8–10, pp. 40–41 in the **Cuaderno de gramática.** ☐ For additional practice, do Activity 4, CD 2 in the **Interactive CD-ROM Tutor.**
Study the expressions in the **Así se dice** box on page 151: telling about what you do during a typical week. You should know how to find out what your friends typically do during the week and how to say what they do typically during the week.	☐ Do Activity 19, p. 152 as a writing activity. Write about your family or circle of friends. ☐ Do Activity 20, p. 152 as a writing activity. Write about yourself. ☐ Do Activity 21, p. 152. ☐ For additional practice, do Activities 7, 8, pp. 162–163 in **Más práctica gramatical.** ☐ For additional practice, do Activity 12, p. 55 in the **Cuaderno de actividades.**

CAPÍTULO 5

■ SEGUNDO PASO Self-Test

Can you talk about what you and your friends like to do together?

How would you ask the following people or groups of people if they like to do each of the following activities? How would each person or group answer you?

1. Franco/to organize his room

2. Cristina y Marta/to run in the park together

3. Gerardo y Esteban/to scuba dive together

4. Pablo/to read novels

5. Linda y Laura/to ski together

6. Daniel/to exercise in the gym

7. Isabel/to write letters

For an **online self-test**, go to **go.hrw.com**.

WV3 FLORIDA–5

CAPÍTULO 5

CAPÍTULO

5 El ritmo de la vida

■ TERCER PASO Student Make-Up Assignments Checklist

Pupil's Edition, pp. 154–157

Study the expressions in the **Así se dice** box on page 154: giving today's date. You should know how to find out today's date, give today's date, and tell on what date something happens.	☐ For additional practice, do Activity 7, p. 162 in **Más práctica gramatical.**
Study the **Vocabulario** on page 154.	☐ For additional practice, do Activities 13–15, p. 56 in the **Cuaderno de actividades.** ☐ For additional practice, do Activity 11, p. 42 in the **Cuaderno de gramática.** ☐ For additional practice, do Activity 6, CD 2 in the **Interactive CD-ROM Tutor.**
Study the grammar presentation in the **Nota gramatical** box on page 154: giving the date.	☐ Do Activity 22, p. 154 as a writing activity. Write down the dates of your favorite holidays and anniversaries. ☐ Do Activity 24, p. 155. ☐ For additional practice, do Activity 7, p. 162 in **Más práctica gramatical.** ☐ For additional practice, do Activities 12–14, pp. 42–43 in the **Cuaderno de gramática.**
Study the expressions in the **Así se dice** box on page 156: talking about the weather. You should know how to find out what the weather is like and how to say what the weather is like.	☐ Do Activity 27, p. 156. ☐ Do Activity 28, p. 157 as a writing activity. ☐ Do Activity 29, p. 157 as a writing activity. Write about yourself. ☐ Do Activity 30, p. 157. ☐ For additional practice, do Activity 9, p. 163 in **Más práctica gramatical.**
Study the **Vocabulario** on page 156.	☐ For additional practice, do Activity 9, p. 163 in **Más práctica gramatical.** ☐ For additional practice, do Activities 15–16, p. 44 in the **Cuaderno de gramática.** ☐ For additional practice, do Activity 5, CD 2 in the **Interactive CD-ROM Tutor.**

CAPÍTULO 5

■ TERCER PASO Self-Test

Can you talk about what you do during a typical week?	How would you tell a classmate about five activities you typically do each week?

Can you give today's date?	How would you tell a classmate the date of the following things?
	1. the Spanish test - March 5
	2. the football game - September 14
	3. John's party - May 1
	4. the school dance - July 29
	5. the jazz concert - January 18

Can you talk about the weather?	How would you describe the weather if it were . . . ?
	1. rainy and cold
	2. a nice, sunny day
	3. cold and windy
	4. snowy
	5. hot and sunny
	6. a cloudy day
	7. cool
	8. a terrible, rainy day
	What would be a typical weather description of your hometown during the following times of the year?
	1. el otoño
	2. el invierno
	3. la primavera
	4. el verano

CAPÍTULO 5

For an **online self-test**, go to **go.hrw.com**.

WV3 FLORIDA–5

CAPÍTULO

6 Entre familia

■ PRIMER PASO Student Make-Up Assignments Checklist

Pupil's Edition, pp. 173–177

Study the **Vocabulario** on page 173.	☐ For additional practice, do Activity 3, p. 62 in the **Cuaderno de actividades**. ☐ For additional practice, do Activities 1–2, p. 45 in the **Cuaderno de gramática**. ☐ For additional practice, do Activity 1, CD 2 in the **Interactive CD-ROM Tutor**.
Study the expressions in the **Así se dice** box on page 174: describing a family. You should know how to find out how often a friend's family and how to talk about your family.	☐ Do Activity 7, p. 174 as a writing activity. Write about your family. ☐ For additional practice, do Activity 2, p. 190 in **Más práctica gramatical**.
Study the grammar presentation in the **Nota gramatical** box on page 174: possessive adjectives.	☐ Do Activity 8, p. 174 as a writing activity. ☐ Do Activity 9, p. 175 as a writing activity. ☐ Do Activity 10, p. 175 as a writing activity. Write sentences about your family. ☐ Do Activity 12, p. 176. ☐ Do Activity 13, p. 176. ☐ Do Activity 14, p. 176 as a writing activity. Answer the questionnaire you created for Activity 13. ☐ For additional practice, do Activities 1–2, p. 190 in **Más práctica gramatical**. ☐ For additional practice, do Activities 3–4, p. 46 in the **Cuaderno de gramática**. ☐ For additional practice, do Activity 2, CD 2 in the **Interactive CD-ROM Tutor**.

CAPÍTULO 6

■ PRIMER PASO Self-Test

| Can you describe a family? | Can you tell Ramiro, a new student at your school . . . ? |

Can you describe a family?

Can you tell Ramiro, a new student at your school . . . ?

1. how many people there are in your family
2. how many brothers and sisters you have
3. what the names of your family members are
4. what they like to do in their free time

For an **online self-test**, go to **go.hrw.com**.

WV3 FLORIDA–6

CAPÍTULO 6

Spanish 1 ¡Ven conmigo!, Chapter 6

■ SEGUNDO PASO Student Make-Up Assignments Checklist

Pupil's Edition, pp. 178–182

Study the expressions in the **Así se dice** box on page 178: describing people. You should know how to ask for a description of someone and how to describe someone.	☐ Do Activity 17, p. 179. ☐ Do Activity 18, p. 179 as a writing activity. Describe a person as fully as possible. ☐ Do Activity 20, p. 179. ☐ For additional practice, do Activity 2, p. 190 in **Más práctica gramatical.** ☐ For additional practice, do Activity 4, CD 2 in the **Interactive CD-ROM Tutor.**
Study the **Vocabulario** on page 178.	☐ For additional practice, do Activities 5–6, p. 47 in the **Cuaderno de gramática.**
Study the expressions in the **Así se dice** box on page 180: discussing things a family does together. You should know how to find out what a family does together and how to say what you and your family do together.	☐ For additional practice, do Activity 6, p. 192 in **Más práctica gramatical.**
Study the grammar presentation in the **Nota gramatical** box on page 180: the verb **hacer.**	☐ Do Activity 22, p. 181. ☐ For additional practice, do Activities 3–5, p. 191 in **Más práctica gramatical.** ☐ For additional practice, do Activity 13, p. 67 in the **Cuaderno de actividades.** ☐ For additional practice, do Activities 8–9, pp. 48–49 in the **Cuaderno de gramática.** ☐ For additional practice, do Activity 3, CD 2 in the **Interactive CD-ROM Tutor.**

C A P Í T U L O 6

Spanish 1 ¡Ven conmigo!, Chapter 6

Student Make-Up Assignments **35**

Study the grammar presentation in the **Nota gramatical** box on page 181: personal **a**.	☐ Do Activity 23, p. 181. ☐ Do Activity 24, p. 181 as a writing activity. ☐ Do Activity 25, p. 182 as a writing activity. Write about your family. ☐ Do Activity 27, p. 182. ☐ For additional practice, do Activity 6, p. 192 in **Más práctica gramatical**. ☐ For additional practice, do Activity 11, p. 66 in the **Cuaderno de actividades**. ☐ For additional practice, do Activity 10, p. 49 in the **Cuaderno de gramática**.

■ SEGUNDO PASO Self-Test

Can you describe what people look like?	Look at the pictures for this activity on page XX and describe the members of Florencia's family. 1. su abuelo 2. su hermano, Toño 3. su mamá 4. su hermano, Óscar
Can you discuss things a family does together?	Write one or two sentences about each member of your family or an imaginary family. Include age, physical description, job, where they live, and what you do with them.

For an **online self-test**, go to **go.hrw.com**.

WV3 FLORIDA–6

CAPÍTULO 6

6 Entre familia

■ TERCER PASO Student Make-Up Assignments Checklist
Pupil's Edition, pp. 184–187

Study the expressions in the **Así se dice** box on page 184: discussing problems and giving advice. You should know how to discuss a problem and how to give advice.	☐ For additional practice, do Activities 7–9, pp. 192–193 in **Más práctica gramatical.**
Study the grammar presentation in the **Nota gramatical** box on page 184: the verb **deber.**	☐ Do Activity 29, p. 184 as a writing activity. ☐ For additional practice, do Activities 7–8, pp. 192–193 in **Más práctica gramatical.** ☐ For additional practice, do Activities 14–15, p. 68 in the **Cuaderno de actividades.** ☐ For additional practice, do Activities 11–12, p. 50 in the **Cuaderno de gramática.**
Study the **Vocabulario** on page 185.	☐ For additional practice, do Activity 7, p. 192 in **Más práctica gramatical.** ☐ For additional practice, do Activities 13–15, p. 51 in the **Cuaderno de gramática.** ☐ For additional practice, do Activity 5, CD 2 in the **Interactive CD-ROM Tutor.**
Study the grammar presentation in the **Nota gramatical** box on page 185: the verb **poner.**	☐ Do Activity 30, p. 185. ☐ Do Activity 31, p. 186 as a writing activity. ☐ Do Activity 32, p. 186 as a writing activity. ☐ Do Activity 33, p. 186 as a writing activity. ☐ Do Activity 35, p. 187 as a writing activity. ☐ Do Activity 36, p. 187. ☐ Do Activity 37, p. 187. ☐ For additional practice, do Activity 9, p. 193 in **Más práctica gramatical.** ☐ For additional practice, do Activities 16–17, p. 52 in the **Cuaderno de gramática.**

CAPÍTULO 6

■ TERCER PASO Self-Test

| Can you discuss problems and give advice? | Paula and her family need help solving these problems. What should each person do? |

Paula and her family need help solving these problems. What should each person do?

1. Her sister is disorganized and can't find any of her things.

2. Paula's brother works all the time, and he's very tired.

3. It's six o'clock in the evening and everyone's hungry.

4. Paula's sister is in trouble at school because she talks too much in class.

 For an **online self-test**, go to **go.hrw.com**.

WV3 FLORIDA–6

CAPÍTULO 7

¿Qué te gustaría hacer?

■ **PRIMER PASO** Student Make-Up Assignments Checklist

Pupil's Edition, pp. 207–211

Study the expressions in the **Así se dice** box on page 207: talking on the telephone. You should know how to make a telephone call and how to leave a message.	☐ Do Activity 7, p. 208. ☐ For additional practice, do Activities 3–4, p. 74 in the **Cuaderno de actividades**. ☐ For additional practice, do Activities 1–2, p. 53 in the **Cuaderno de gramática**.
Study the expressions in the **Así se dice** box on page 208: extending and accepting invitations. You should know how to invite a friend to do something and how to accept an invitation.	☐ For additional practice, do Activities 3–4, p. 46 in the **Cuaderno de gramática**. ☐ For additional practice, do Activity 2, CD 2 in the **Interactive CD-ROM Tutor**.
Study the grammar presentation in the **Gramática** box on page 209: **e → ie** stem-changing verbs.	☐ Do Activity 10, p. 209. ☐ Do Activity 11, p. 209. ☐ Do Activity 13, p. 211 as a writing activity. ☐ Do Activity 14, p. 211 as a writing activity. ☐ Do Activity 15, p. 211. ☐ For additional practice, do Activities 1–2, p. 222 in **Más práctica gramatical**. ☐ For additional practice, do Activities 3–4, p. 54 in the **Cuaderno de gramática**. ☐ For additional practice, do Activity 2, CD 2 in the **Interactive CD-ROM Tutor**.
Study the **Vocabulario** on page 210.	☐ Do Activity 13, p. 211 as a writing activity. Write a conversation based on the clues from the activity. ☐ Do Activity 14, p. 211 as a writing activity. ☐ Do Activity 15, p. 211. ☐ For additional practice, do Activities 5–7, p. 55 in the **Cuaderno de gramática**. ☐ For additional practice, do Activity 1, CD 2 in the **Interactive CD-ROM Tutor**.

■ PRIMER PASO Self-Test

Can you talk on the telephone?	You're answering phones at the office at your school. What would you say in the following situation?

El teléfono suena.

TÚ _____

EL SR. GIBSON Buenas tardes. ¿Está la profesora Margarita Gibson, por favor?

TÚ _____

EL SR. GIBSON De parte de su esposo.

TÚ _____

EL SR. GIBSON ¿Puedo dejar un recado?

TÚ _____

Can you extend and accept invitations?	How would you invite the following people to do something with you? How might they accept your invitation?

1. tu mejor amigo/a

2. tu hermano/a

3. uno de tus padres

4. tu profesor/a

5. tu primo/a

6. tu novio/a

 For an **online self-test**, go to **go.hrw.com**.

WV3 ECUADOR–7

7 ¿Qué te gustaría hacer?

Nombre _____ Clase _____ Fecha _____

■ SEGUNDO PASO Student Make-Up Assignments Checklist

Pupil's Edition, pp. 212–215

Study the expressions in the **Así se dice** box on page 212: making plans. You should know how to talk about making plans.	☐ For additional practice, do Activities 3–4, p. 223 in **Más práctica gramatical**.
Study the grammar presentation in the **Nota gramatical** box on page 212: the verb **pensar**, and the structure **ir + a**.	☐ Do Activity 16, p. 212. ☐ Do Activity 17, p. 213. ☐ Do Activity 18, p. 213 as a writing activity. Write about yourself. ☐ For additional practice, do Activity 5, p. 224 in **Más práctica gramatical**. ☐ For additional practice, do Activities 9–10, pp. 77–78 in the **Cuaderno de actividades**. ☐ For additional practice, do Activities 8–11, pp. 56–57 in the **Cuaderno de gramática**. ☐ For additional practice, do Activity 3, CD 2 in the **Interactive CD-ROM Tutor**.
Study the expressions in the **Así se dice** box on page 214: talking about getting ready. You should know how to ask if a friend is ready and how to say if you are ready.	☐ For additional practice, do Activity 6, p. 224 in **Más práctica gramatical**. ☐ For additional practice, do Activity 4, CD 2 in the **Interactive CD-ROM Tutor**.
Study the grammar presentation in the **Nota gramatical** box on page 214: reflexive verbs.	☐ Do Activity 20, p. 214 as a writing activity. Write about your daily routine. ☐ Do Activity 21, p. 215. ☐ Do Activity 22, p. 215 as a writing activity. ☐ Do Activity 23, p. 215 as a writing activity. ☐ For additional practice, do Activity 6, p. 224 in **Más práctica gramatical**. ☐ For additional practice, do Activities 12–13, p. 58 in the **Cuaderno de gramática**.

■ SEGUNDO PASO Self-Test

Can you make plans?	What do you plan to do this weekend? Give specific days, times, and places you plan to go, people you plan to see, and things you plan to do.
Can you talk about getting ready?	What do you usually need to do to get ready in these situations? 1. para ir al colegio 2. para salir con amigos 3. para ir a una fiesta formal 4. para ir a una boda 5. para hacer un viaje al campo 6. para ir al teatro

 For an **online self-test**, go to **go.hrw.com**.

WV3 ECUADOR–7

CAPÍTULO 7

7 ¿Qué te gustaría hacer?

■ TERCER PASO Student Make-Up Assignments Checklist
Pupil's Edition, pp. 217–219

Study the expressions in the **Así se dice** box on page 217: turning down an invitation and explaining why. You should know how to turn down an invitation.	☐ For additional practice, do Activity 7, p. 225 in **Más práctica gramatical**. ☐ For additional practice, do Activities 14–15, p. 59 in the **Cuaderno de gramática**. ☐ For additional practice, do Activity 5, CD 2 in the **Interactive CD-ROM Tutor**.
Study the grammar presentation in the **Nota gramatical** box on page 217: expressions with **tener**.	☐ Do Activity 25, p. 218. ☐ Do Activity 26, p. 218 as a writing activity. ☐ Do Activity 27, p. 218. ☐ Do Activity 28, p. 219 as a writing activity. ☐ Do Activity 29, p. 219. ☐ For additional practice, do Activity 8, p. 225 in **Más práctica gramatical**. ☐ For additional practice, do Activities 15–17, pp. 81–82 in the **Cuaderno de actividades**. ☐ For additional practice, do Activities 16–17, p. 60 **Cuaderno de gramática**. ☐ For additional practice, do Activity 6, CD 2 in the **Interactive CD-ROM Tutor**.

CAPÍTULO 7

◼ TERCER PASO Self-Test

Can you turn down an invitation and explain why?	How would you turn down the following invitations?
	1. Your friend invites you to a surprise birthday party for his four-year-old brother.
	2. Your parents invite you to go to the theater with them.
	3. Your teacher invites you and your parents to go to the amusement park with him and his family.
	Regina is a new girl at school, and Samuel wants to get to know her better. Unfortunately, she has a different excuse for everything he asks her to do. What are some of her excuses?
	1. Regina, ¿quieres ir al partido de béisbol del colegio el viernes después de clase?
	2. ¿Quieres ir al zoológico el sábado?
	3. Entonces, ¿te gustaría estudiar juntos el domingo por la tarde?

  For an **online self-test**, go to **go.hrw.com**.

WV3 ECUADOR–7

CAPÍTULO

8 ¡A comer!

■ PRIMER PASO Student Make-Up Assignments Checklist

Pupil's Edition, pp. 235–238

Study the expressions in the **Así se dice** box on page 235: talking about meals and food. You should know how to ask your friend about meals and food and how to say what you like to eat.	☐ For additional practice, do Activities 1, 3, p. 252, 253 in **Más práctica gramatical**.
Study the **Vocabulario** on page 235.	☐ For additional practice, do Activities 1–2, p. 61 in the **Cuaderno de gramática**.
Study the grammar presentation in the **Gramática** box on page 236: the verb **encantar** and indirect object pronouns.	☐ Do Activity 7, p. 236. ☐ Do Activity 8, p. 236 as a writing activity. ☐ Do Activity 9, p. 237. ☐ Do Activity 10, p. 237. ☐ For additional practice, do Activity 2, p. 252 in **Más práctica gramatical**. ☐ For additional practice, do Activities 3–4, p. 62 in the **Cuaderno de gramática**.
Study the **Vocabulario** on page 237.	☐ For additional practice, do Activity 7, p. 88 in the **Cuaderno de actividades**. ☐ For additional practice, do Activities 5–6, p. 63 in the **Cuaderno de gramática**. ☐ For additional practice, do Activity 2, CD 2 in the **Interactive CD-ROM Tutor**.
Study the grammar presentation in the **Gramática** box on page 238: o → ue stem-changing verbs.	☐ Do Activity 13, p. 238 as a writing activity. ☐ Do the first part of Activity 14, p. 238. Write three sentences about your family members. ☐ For additional practice, do Activity 4, p. 253 in **Más práctica gramatical**. ☐ For additional practice, do Activities 7–8, p. 64 in the **Cuaderno de gramática**. ☐ For additional practice, do Activity 1, CD 2 in the **Interactive CD-ROM Tutor**.

■ PRIMER PASO Self-Test

Can you talk about meals and food? How would you tell a classmate what your favorite breakfast foods are?

How would you ask what he or she usually eats for breakfast? How would you tell a classmate what you eat for breakfast . . . ?

1. on weekends

2. when you're very hungry

3. when you're in a big hurry

4. when someone takes you out for breakfast

5. on school days

How would you tell a classmate what you have for lunch and ask what he or she has for lunch?

 For an **online self-test**, go to **go.hrw.com**.

WV3 ECUADOR–7

Spanish 1 ¡Ven conmigo!, Chapter 8

¡A comer!

■ SEGUNDO PASO Student Make-Up Assignments Checklist

Pupil's Edition, pp. 240–242

Study the expressions in the **Así se dice** box on page 240: commenting on food. You should know how to ask how something tastes and say how something tastes.	☐ For additional practice, do Activities 1–3, pp. 252–253 in **Más práctica gramatical**. ☐ For additional practice, do Activity 3, CD 2 in the **Interactive CD-ROM Tutor**.
Study the grammar presentation in the **Nota gramatical** box on page 240: the verbs **ser** and **estar**.	☐ Do Activity 18, p. 241. ☐ Do Activity 20, p. 241 as a writing activity. ☐ For additional practice, do Activities 5–6, p. 254 in **Más práctica gramatical**. ☐ For additional practice, do Activities 11, p. 90 in the **Cuaderno de actividades**. ☐ For additional practice, do Activities 9–10, p. 65 in the **Cuaderno de gramática**.
Study the grammar presentation in the **Nota gramatical** box on page 241: more expressions with **tener**.	☐ Do Activity 22, p. 242. ☐ Do Activity 23, p. 242 as a writing activity. ☐ Do Activity 24, p. 242 as a writing activity. ☐ Do Activity 25, p. 242. ☐ For additional practice, do Activity 7, pp. 254–255 in **Más práctica gramatical**. ☐ For additional practice, do Activities 11–12, p. 66 in the **Cuaderno de gramática**.

C A P Í T U L O 8

■ SEGUNDO PASO Self-Test

| Can you comment on food? | Look at the pictures of Activity 3 in the **A ver si puedo...** for this chapter on page 258. Can you write a sentence describing how you think each dish tastes? |

For an **online self-test**, go to **go.hrw.com**.

WV3 ECUADOR–8

CAPÍTULO 8

CAPÍTULO

8 ¡A comer!

■ TERCER PASO Student Make-Up Assignments Checklist

Pupil's Edition, pp. 244–249

Study the expressions in the **Así se dice** box on page 244: making polite requests. You should know how to ask the waitperson to bring you something.	☐ For additional practice, do Activity 8, p. 255 in **Más práctica gramatical**.
Study the **Vocabulario** on page 244.	☐ For additional practice, do Activities 13–15, p. 67 in the **Cuaderno de gramática**.
Study the grammar presentation in the **Nota gramatical** box on page 244: forms of **otro**.	☐ Do Activity 26, p. 244. ☐ For additional practice, do Activities 16–17, p. 68 in the **Cuaderno de gramática**.
Study the **Vocabulario** on page 245.	☐ Do Activity 27, p. 245. ☐ For additional practice, do Activity 9, p. 255 in **Más práctica gramatical**. ☐ For additional practice, do Activities 15–16, pp. 92–93 in the **Cuaderno de actividades**. ☐ For additional practice, do Activities 18–19, p. 69 in the **Cuaderno de gramática**. ☐ For additional practice, do Activity 4, CD 2 in the **Interactive CD-ROM Tutor**.
Study the expressions in the **Así se dice** box on page 246: ordering dinner in a restaurant. You should know how to find out what a friend is going to order and say what you are going to order.	☐ Do Activity 29, p. 246 as a writing activity. ☐ Do the first part of Activity 30, p. 246. ☐ For additional practice, do Activity 8, p. 255 in **Más práctica gramatical**.
Study the expressions in the **Así se dice** box on page 246: asking for and paying the bill in a restaurant. You should know how to function in a restaurant.	☐ Do Activity 33, p. 248. ☐ Do Activity 34, p. 248 as a writing activity. ☐ Do Activity 35, p. 249 as a writing activity. ☐ For additional practice, do Activity 6, CD 2 in the **Interactive CD-ROM Tutor**.

Study the **Vocabulario** on page 247.	☐ Do Activity 31, p. 247 as a writing activity.
	☐ For additional practice, do Activity 9, p. 255 in **Más práctica gramatical**.
	☐ For additional practice, do Activities 20–21, p. 69 in the **Cuaderno de gramática**.
	☐ For additional practice, do Activity 5, CD 2 in the **Interactive CD-ROM Tutor**.

■ TERCER PASO Self-Test

Can you make polite requests?	You're eating with your family in a restaurant in Ecuador, and you're the only one who speaks Spanish. How would you ask the wait-person . . . ?
	1. to bring spoons for everyone
	2. to bring you a knife and a napkin
	3. to bring another menu
	4. to bring you a clean glass
Can you order dinner in a restaurant?	Imagine you and a friend are at El Rancho Restaurant.
	1. How would you ask your friend what he or she is going to order?
	2. How would you tell the waitperson that you want to order a salad?
Can you ask for and pay the bill in a restaurant?	How would you ask the waitperson how much the meal is? How would you ask him or her to bring you the bill?

CAPÍTULO 8

 For an **online self-test**, go to **go.hrw.com**.

WV3 ECUADOR–8

CAPÍTULO 9

¡Vamos de compras!

■ PRIMER PASO Student Make-Up Assignments Checklist

Pupil's Edition, pp. 269–272

Study the expressions in the **Así se dice** box on page 269: discussing gift suggestions. You should know how to find out what gift a friend has in mind for someone and how to say what gift you have in mind for someone.	☐ Do Activity 7, p. 270. ☐ For additional practice, do Activity 1, p. 284 in **Más práctica gramatical.** ☐ For additional practice, do Activity 3, p. 98 in the **Cuaderno de actividades.** ☐ For additional practice, do Activity 2, CD 3 in the **Interactive CD-ROM Tutor.**
Study the **Vocabulario** on page 269.	☐ For additional practice, do Activities 1–2, pp. 284-285 in **Más práctica gramatical.** ☐ For additional practice, do Activities 1–2, p. 70 in the **Cuaderno de gramática.** ☐ For additional practice, do Activity 1, CD 3 in the **Interactive CD-ROM Tutor.**
Study the grammar presentation in the **Gramática** box on page 270: indirect object pronouns.	☐ Do Activity 8, p. 270. ☐ Do Activity 9, p. 270 as a writing activity. ☐ For additional practice, do Activity 2, p. 284 in **Más práctica gramatical.** ☐ For additional practice, do Activities 3–5, pp. 71–72 in the **Cuaderno de gramática.**
Study the expressions in the **Así se dice** box on page 271: asking for and giving directions downtown. You should know how to find out where a shop is located and how to say where a shop is located.	☐ Do Activity 10, p. 271 as a writing activity. Write a description of Río Blanco.
Study the **Vocabulario** on page 271.	☐ Do Activity 12, p. 272 as a writing activity. ☐ Do Activity 13, p. 272 as a writing activity. ☐ Do Activity 14, p. 272 as a writing activity. ☐ For additional practice, do Activities 17–18, p. 73 in the **Cuaderno de gramática.**

CAPÍTULO 9

■ PRIMER PASO Self-Test

Can you discuss gift suggestions?	You and a friend are shopping for a birthday gift for your Spanish teacher. How would you ask your friend about what you should get for your teacher? How might he or she make a suggestion?
Can you ask for and give directions downtown?	Imagine you're at the supermarket on the map of Activity 2 in the **A ver si puedo...** for this chapter on page 290 of your textbook. Can you ask someone where the restaurant and the hospital are? How would he or she answer?

For an **online self-test**, go to **go.hrw.com**.

WV3 TEXAS–9

CAPÍTULO 9

CAPÍTULO 9 ¡Vamos de compras!

■ SEGUNDO PASO Student Make-Up Assignments Checklist

Pupil's Edition, pp. 274–278

Study the expressions in the **Así se dice** box on page 274: commenting on clothes. You should know how to find out what someone is going to wear and how to say what you are going to wear.	☐ Activity 16, p. 275. ☐ Do Activity 18, p. 275 as a writing activity. ☐ For additional practice, do Activity 3, p. 285 in **Más práctica gramatical.**
Study the **Vocabulario** on page 274.	☐ For additional practice, do Activities 3–4, p. 285 in **Más práctica gramatical.** ☐ For additional practice, do Activities 9–10, p. 74 in the **Cuaderno de gramática.** ☐ For additional practice, do Activity 4, CD 3 in the **Interactive CD-ROM Tutor.**
Study the grammar presentation in the **Nota gramatical** box on page 275: **ser + de +** material or pattern.	☐ Do Activity 19, p. 276 as a writing activity. ☐ Do Activity 20, p. 276. ☐ Do Activity 21, p. 277 as a writing activity. Write about your preferences. ☐ Do Activity 22, p. 277 as a writing activity. ☐ For additional practice, do Activity 4, p. 285 in **Más práctica gramatical.** ☐ For additional practice, do Activities 11–12, p. 75 in the **Cuaderno de gramática.**
Study the **Vocabulario** on page 275.	☐ For additional practice, do Activities 3–4, 6–8, pp. 285–287 in **Más práctica gramatical.** ☐ For additional practice, do Activities 7–8, p. 101 in the **Cuaderno de actividades.**
Study the expressions in the **Así se dice** box on page 277: making comparisons. You should know how to compare things.	☐ For additional practice, do Activity 5, p. 286 in **Más práctica gramatical.**

CAPÍTULO 9

| Study the grammar presentation in the **Gramática** box on page 277: making comparisons. | ☐ Do Activity 23, p. 277 as a writing activity. ☐ Do Activity 25, p. 278. ☐ For additional practice, do Activity 5, p. 286 in **Más práctica gramatical**. ☐ For additional practice, do Activities 13–14, p. 76 in the **Cuaderno de gramática**. ☐ For additional practice, do Activity 3, CD 3 in the **Interactive CD-ROM Tutor**. |

■ SEGUNDO PASO Self-Test

| Can you comment on clothes? | How would you describe the clothes you're wearing right now? Describe the color, pattern, and material of each item. |
| Can you make comparisons? | Look at the drawings in Activity 4 of the **A ver si puedo...** for this chapter on page 290 of your textbook. How would you compare the two items in each drawing? |

For an **online self-test**, go to **go.hrw.com**.

WV3 TEXAS–9

CAPÍTULO 9 ¡Vamos de compras!

■ TERCER PASO Student Make-Up Assignments Checklist

Pupil's Edition, pp. 279–281

Study the expressions in the **Así se dice** box on page 279: expressing preferences. You should know how to find out what item a friend prefers and say what item you prefer.	☐ For additional practice, do Activities 6–7, pp. 286–287 in **Más práctica gramatical**.
Study the grammar presentation in the **Nota gramatical** box on page 279: demonstrative adjectives.	☐ Do Activity 26, p. 279. ☐ Do Activity 27, p. 279 as a writing activity. ☐ Do Activity 28, p. 279 as a writing activity. ☐ For additional practice, do Activities 11–13, p. 104 in the **Cuaderno de actividades**. ☐ For additional practice, do Activities 15–16, p. 77 in the **Cuaderno de gramática**. ☐ For additional practice, do Activity 6, CD 3 in the **Interactive CD-ROM Tutor**.
Study the expressions in the **Así se dice** box on page 280: asking about prices and paying for something. You should know how to ask how much one or more items cost and say how much an item costs.	☐ Do Activity 30, p. 281 as a writing activity. ☐ Do Activity 31, p. 281 as a writing activity. ☐ Do Activity 32, p. 281. ☐ For additional practice, do Activity 8, p. 287 in **Más práctica gramatical**. ☐ For additional practice, do Activities 17–18, p. 78 in the **Cuaderno de gramática**. ☐ For additional practice, do Activity 5, CD 3 in the **Interactive CD-ROM Tutor**.
Study the **Vocabulario** on page 280.	☐ Do Activity 19, p. 78 in the **Cuaderno de gramática**.

CAPÍTULO 9

◼ TERCER PASO Self-Test

Can you express preferences?	Look at the pictures in Activity 4 in the **A ver si puedo...** for this chapter on page 290 in the textbook. For each pair of items, tell which one you prefer and why.
Can you ask about prices and pay for something?	You're in a shopping center in Mexico and the salesclerk doesn't speak English. How would you ask the prices of the following items? How might the clerk answer? a. a yellow cotton blouse b. a silk tie c. chocolate candies d. a greeting card

 For an **online self-test**, go to **go.hrw.com**.

WV3 TEXAS–9

CAPÍTULO 10

Celebraciones

■ PRIMER PASO Student Make-Up Assignments Checklist

Pupil's Edition, pp. 297–300

Study the **Vocabulario** on page 297.	☐ Do Activity 6, p. 297.
	☐ Do Activity 8, p. 298 as a writing activity.
	☐ For additional practice, do Activity 1, p. 314 in **Más práctica gramatical**.
	☐ For additional practice, do Activity 1, p. 79 in the **Cuaderno de gramática**.
	☐ For additional practice, do Activity 1, CD 3 in the **Interactive CD-ROM Tutor**.
Study the expressions in the **Así se dice** box on page 298: talking about what you're doing right now. You should know how to find out what someone is doing right now and say what you are doing right now.	☐ For additional practice, do Activities 2–3, pp. 314–315 in **Más práctica gramatical**.
Study the grammar presentation in the **Gramática** box on page 299: present progressive.	☐ Do Activity 10, p. 299 as a writing activity. Write what the people in all the pictures are doing.
	☐ Do Activity 11, p. 299.
	☐ Do Activity 12, p. 300 as a writing activity. Write the phone conversation between the two friends.
	☐ For additional practice, do Activities 2–3, pp. 314–315 in **Más práctica gramatical**.
	☐ For additional practice, do Activities 2–6, pp. 80–81 in the **Cuaderno de gramática**.
	☐ For additional practice, do Activity 2, CD 3 in the **Interactive CD-ROM Tutor**.
Study the expressions in the **Así se dice** box on page 300: asking for and giving an opinion. You should know how to find out what a friend thinks about something and say what you think about something.	☐ Do Activity 13, p. 300 as a writing activity.
	☐ Do Activity 14, p. 300 as a writing activity. Write what you think about the holidays.
	☐ Do Activity 15, p. 300 as a writing activity.
	☐ Do Activity 16, p. 300.

CAPÍTULO 10

■ PRIMER PASO Self-Test

Can you talk about what you're doing right now?	Imagine that today is one of the following holidays. How would you tell a friend on the phone what you're doing right now?
	1. la Navidad
	2. el Día de Acción de Gracias
	How would you say that . . . ?
	1. Héctor is opening gifts
	2. Manuel is buying the cake
	3. Rebeca is calling the guests
	4. Mario and Juan are decorating the living room
	5. Grandmother is preparing the tamales
	6. we are all eating and drinking
	7. Aníbal is talking on the phone
	8. Eva and Lisa are blowing up balloons
Can you ask for and give an opinion?	How would you ask a guest what she or he thinks of . . . ?
	1. the party
	2. the food
	3. the music
	4. the dessert

 For an **online self-test**, go to **go.hrw.com**.

WV3 TEXAS–10

Spanish 1 ¡Ven conmigo!, Chapter 10

CAPÍTULO 10

Celebraciones

■ SEGUNDO PASO Student Make-Up Assignments Checklist

Pupil's Edition, pp. 302–305

Study the expressions in the **Así se dice** box on page 302: asking for help and responding to requests. You should know how to ask for help and say you agree to help or refuse polite to help.	☐ Do Activity 17, p. 302 as a writing activity. ☐ Do Activity 19, p. 303 as a writing activity. ☐ Do Activity 20, p. 303. ☐ Do Activity 21, p. 303 as a writing activity. Use the questions from Activity 20 to write a conversation in which you ask for help. ☐ For additional practice, do Activities 4–5, pp. 315–316 in **Más práctica gramatical**.
Study the **Vocabulario** on page 302.	☐ For additional practice, do Activities 4–5, pp. 315–316 in **Más práctica gramatical**. ☐ For additional practice, do Activities 7–8, p. 82 in the **Cuaderno de gramática**. ☐ For additional practice, do Activity 4, CD 3 in the **Interactive CD-ROM Tutor**.
Study the expressions in the **Así se dice** box on page 304: telling a friend what to do. You should know how to tell a friend what to do and say you agree to do something.	☐ For additional practice, do Activity 5, p. 316 in **Más práctica gramatical**.
Study the grammar presentation in the **Nota gramatical** box on page 304: informal commands.	☐ Do Activity 23, p. 304. ☐ Do Activity 24, p. 305 as a writing activity. Write a conversation in which you tell your friend politely to do certain things. ☐ Do Activity 25, p. 305. ☐ Do Activity 26, p. 305 as a writing activity. Write a conversation in which you tell your friend politely to do the things you listed in Activity 25. ☐ For additional practice, do Activity 5, p. 316 in **Más práctica gramatical**. ☐ For additional practice, do Activities 10–12, pp. 114–115 in the **Cuaderno de actividades**.

CAPÍTULO 10

☐ For additional practice, do Activities 9–12, pp. 83–84 in the **Cuaderno de gramática.**

☐ For additional practice, do Activity 3, CD 3 in the **Interactive CD-ROM Tutor.**

■ SEGUNDO PASO Self-Test

Can you ask for help and respond to requests?	The Spanish Club is planning an end-of-the-year party. Can you write notes to five club members asking for their help in completing the preparations?
Can you tell a friend what to do?	How would you tell a friend to do the following things? 1. study more 2. do your homework 3. organize your room 4. read your book 5. eat more vegetables 6. do exercises 7. attend class every day 8. help at home

 For an **online self-test**, go to **go.hrw.com.**

WV3 TEXAS–10

Spanish 1 ¡Ven conmigo!, Chapter 10

CAPÍTULO 10

Celebraciones

■ TERCER PASO Student Make-Up Assignments Checklist

Pupil's Edition, pp. 307–311

Study the expressions in the **Así se dice** box on page 307: talking about past events. You should know how to find out what a friend did and say what you did.	☐ For additional practice, do Activities 6–7, pp. 316–317 in **Más práctica gramatical.**

Study the **Vocabulario** on page 307.	☐ For additional practice, do Activities 16–17, p. 86 in the **Cuaderno de gramática.**

Study the grammar presentation in the **Nota gramatical** box on page 307: the preterite of regular -**ar** verbs.	☐ Do Activity 27, p. 307.
	☐ Do Activity 29, p. 308 as a writing activity. Write about yourself.
	☐ Do Activity 30, p. 308.
	☐ Do Activity 31, p. 309 as a writing activity.
	☐ Do Activity 32, p. 309 as a writing activity.
	☐ Do Activity 33, p. 309 as a writing activity.
	☐ For additional practice, do Activity 6, p. 316 in **Más práctica gramatical.**
	☐ For additional practice, do Activities 13–15, pp. 85–86 in the **Cuaderno de gramática.**
	☐ For additional practice, do Activity 5, CD 3 in the **Interactive CD-ROM Tutor.**

Study the grammar presentation in the **Nota gramatical** box on page 310: direct object pronouns.	☐ Do Activity 34, p. 310 as a writing activity. Write about yourself.
	☐ Do Activity 35, p. 310 as a writing activity.
	☐ Do Activity 36, p. 310 as a writing activity. Write about yourself.
	☐ Do Activity 37, p. 311 as a writing activity. Write about yourself.
	☐ Do Activity 38, p. 311.
	☐ For additional practice, do Activity 8, p. 317 in **Más práctica gramatical.**

Spanish 1 ¡Ven conmigo!, Chapter 10

☐ For additional practice, do Activity 16, p. 117 in the **Cuaderno de actividades.**

☐ For additional practice, do Activities 18–21, pp. 87–88 in the **Cuaderno de gramática.**

☐ For additional practice, do Activity 6, CD 3 in the **Interactive CD-ROM Tutor**

■ TERCER PASO Self-Test

| Can you talk about past events? | Look at the drawings in Activity 6 on the **A ver si puedo...** page for this chapter (p. 320). Can you write a sentence for each drawing saying what these people did last night? Use your imagination and create a name for each person. |

For an **online self-test**, go to **go.hrw.com**.

WV3 TEXAS–10

Para vivir bien

■ PRIMER PASO Student Make-Up Assignments Checklist

Pupil's Edition, pp. 331–333

Study the expressions in the **Así se dice** box on page 331: making suggestions and expressing feelings. You should know how to suggest something to a friend, ask how a friend is feeling, and answer such questions.	☐ For additional practice, do Activities 1–2, p. 348 in **Más práctica gramatical.** ☐ For additional practice, do Activity 4, p. 122 in the **Cuaderno de actividades.**
Study the grammar presentation in the **Nota gramatical** box on page 331: the verb **sentirse,** a reciprocal verb.	☐ Do Activity 7, p. 332 as a writing activity. ☐ Do Activity 10, p. 333. ☐ Do Activity 12, p. 333. ☐ For additional practice, do Activities 1–2, p. 348 in **Más práctica gramatical.** ☐ For additional practice, do Activities 1–2, p. 89 in the **Cuaderno de gramática.** ☐ For additional practice, do Activity 1, CD 3 in the **Interactive CD-ROM Tutor.**
Study the **Vocabulario** on page 332.	☐ Do Activity 8, p. 332 as a writing activity. Write about the activities you like. ☐ Do Activity 9, p. 332. ☐ For additional practice, do Activity 4, p. 349 in **Más práctica gramatical.** ☐ For additional practice, do Activities 3–4, p. 90 in the **Cuaderno de gramática.** ☐ For additional practice, do Activity 2, CD 3 in the **Interactive CD-ROM Tutor.**

■ **PRIMER PASO** Self-Test

| Can you make suggestions and express feelings? | Look at the drawings on the **A ver si puedo...** page for this chapter (p. 354). Can you tell what each person does to lead a healthy life? |

Look at the drawings on the **A ver si puedo...** page for this chapter (p. 354). Can you tell what each person does to lead a healthy life?

What would you suggest to the following people who want to live a healthy life?

1. tus padres

2. tu mejor amigo/a

3. tu profesor/a

4. tu hermano/a

5. tu novio/a

6. tu primo/a

CAPÍTULO 11

 For an **online self-test**, go to **go.hrw.com**.

WV3 PUERTO RICO–11

Para vivir bien

■ SEGUNDO PASO Student Make-Up Assignments Checklist

Pupil's Edition, pp. 334–338

Study the expressions in the **Así se dice** box on page 334: talking about moods and physical condition. You should know how to find out what kind of mood or condition a friend is in and say how you are.	☐ Do Activity 14, p. 335. ☐ Do Activity 15, p. 335 as a writing activity. ☐ For additional practice, do Activity 6, p. 350 in **Más práctica gramatical**.
Study the **Vocabulario** on page 334.	☐ For additional practice, do Activities 5–7, pp. 91–92 in the **Cuaderno de gramática**. ☐ For additional practice, do Activity 3, CD 3 in the **Interactive CD-ROM Tutor**.
Study the **Vocabulario** on page 335.	☐ For additional practice, do Activity 5, p. 349 in **Más práctica gramatical**. ☐ For additional practice, do Activities 8–9, p. 92 in the **Cuaderno de gramática**. ☐ For additional practice, do Activity 4, CD 3 in the **Interactive CD-ROM Tutor**.
Study the grammar presentation in the **Nota gramatical** box on page 336: the verb **doler**.	☐ Do Activity 18, p. 336. ☐ Do Activity 19, p. 336 as a writing activity. ☐ Do Activity 20, p. 337 as a writing activity. Write about how you feel. ☐ Do Activity 21, p. 337 as a writing activity. ☐ Do Activity 22, p. 337 as a writing activity. ☐ For additional practice, do Activity 6, p. 350 in **Más práctica gramatical**. ☐ For additional practice, do Activities 10–11, p. 93 in the **Cuaderno de gramática**.

■ SEGUNDO PASO Self-Test

Can you talk about moods and physical condition?

Write a sentence telling how you feel in these situations.

1. cuando corres mucho
2. cuando comes muy rápido
3. cuando trabajas demasiado
4. cuando lees mucho
5. cuando estudias seis horas
6. cuando recibes una mala nota
7. cuando tienes tos
8. cuando hace mucho frío
9. cuando escribes exámenes todo el día
10. cuando no estudias para un examen

What parts of the body do you use in these activities?

1. patinar
2. preparar la cena
3. bailar
4. dibujar
5. hablar por teléfono
6. nadar
7. cantar
8. esquiar
9. escuchar música
10. leer

 For an **online self-test**, go to **go.hrw.com**.

WV3 PUERTO RICO–11

Spanish 1 ¡Ven conmigo!, Chapter 11

CAPÍTULO **11**

Para vivir bien

■ TERCER PASO Student Make-Up Assignments Checklist

Pupil's Edition, pp. 340–344

Study the expressions in the **Así se dice** box on page 340: saying what you did. You should know how to find out what a friend did last night and say what you did.	☐ For additional practice, do Activities 7–9, pp. 350–351 in **Más práctica gramatical.** ☐ For additional practice, do Activity 5, CD 3 in the **Interactive CD-ROM Tutor.**
Study the grammar presentation in the **Nota gramatical** box on page 340: the preterite of **jugar.**	☐ Do Activity 26, p. 340. ☐ Do Activity 27, p. 340 as a writing activity. ☐ Do Activity 28, p. 341 as a writing activity. Write about what your family did. ☐ Do Activity 29, p. 341. ☐ For additional practice, do Activities 7–8, pp. 350–351 in **Más práctica gramatical.** ☐ For additional practice, do Activities 12–13, p. 94 in the **Cuaderno de gramática.** ☐ For additional practice, do Activity 6, CD 3 in the **Interactive CD-ROM Tutor.**
Study the expressions in the **Así se dice** box on page 342: talking about where you went and when. You should know how to ask where someone went, talk about different times in the past, and say what you did.	☐ For additional practice, do Activity 8, p. 351 in **Más práctica gramatical.**
Study the grammar presentation in the **Nota gramatical** box on page 342: the preterite of the verb **ir.**	☐ Do Activity 31, p. 342. ☐ Do Activity 32, p. 343 as a writing activity. Write about where you went last week. ☐ For additional practice, do Activity 9, p. 351 in **Más práctica gramatical.** ☐ For additional practice, do Activities 11–12, pp. 128–129 in the **Cuaderno de actividades.** ☐ For additional practice, do Activities 14–16, p. 95 in the **Cuaderno de gramática.**

CAPÍTULO 11

Study the **Vocabulario** on page 343.	☐ Do Activity 34, p. 343.
	☐ Do Activity 35, p. 344 as a writing activity.
	☐ For additional practice, do Activity 8, p. 351 in **Más práctica gramatical**.
	☐ For additional practice, do Activities 17–18, p. 96 in the **Cuaderno de gramática**.

■ TERCER PASO Self-Test

Can you say what you did and talk about where you went and when?	For each combination below, write a sentence telling where the person or persons went and what they did at each location.
	1. Roberto/la piscina
	2. Silvia y Sofía/ la cancha de tenis
	3. La familia Pérez/el campo de fútbol
	4. Mi hermana y yo/la tienda de discos
	5. Tú/el estadio
	6. Mónica y Gabi/la biblioteca
	7. Federico y sus padres/el parque
	8. Yo/el gimnasio

 For an **online self-test**, go to **go.hrw.com**.

WV3 PUERTO RICO–11

CAPÍTULO 11

CAPÍTULO 12

Las vacaciones ideales

■ PRIMER PASO Student Make-Up Assignments Checklist

Pupil's Edition, pp. 361–364

Study the expressions in the **Así se dice** box on page 361: talking about what you do and like to do every day. You should know how to find out what someone does on a regular basis, their routine, and say what you do on a regular basis.	☐ Do Activity 6, p. 361. ☐ For additional practice, do Activities 1–3, p. 376 in **Más práctica gramatical.**
Study the grammar presentation in the **Gramática** box on page 362: stem-changing verbs.	☐ Do Activity 7, p. 362 as a writing activity. ☐ Do Activity 8, p. 362 as a writing activity. Write about yourself. ☐ Do Activity 9, p. 362 as a writing activity. Write about yourself. ☐ For additional practice, do Activities 1–3, p. 376 in **Más práctica gramatical.** ☐ For additional practice, do Activities 1–3, pp. 97–98 in the **Cuaderno de gramática.** ☐ For additional practice, do Activity 2, CD 3 in the **Interactive CD-ROM Tutor.**
Study the expressions in the **Así se dice** box on page 362: making future plans. You should say what a friend is planning to do and what you are planning to do.	☐ For additional practice, do Activity 5, p. 377 in **Más práctica gramatical.**
Study the **Vocabulario** on page 363.	☐ Do the first part of Activity 11, p. 363 as a writing activity. ☐ For additional practice, do Activity 6, p. 136 in the **Cuaderno de actividades.** ☐ For additional practice, do Activities 4–7, pp. 99–100 in the **Cuaderno de gramática.** ☐ For additional practice, do Activity 1, CD 3 in the **Interactive CD-ROM Tutor.**
Study the grammar presentation in the **Gramática** box on page 363: verbs + infinitives.	☐ Do Activity 12, p. 363 as a writing activity. ☐ Do Activity 13, p. 364 as a writing activity. ☐ Do Activity 14, p. 364 as a writing activity. ☐ Do Activity 15, p. 364 as a writing activity.

☐ Do Activity 16, p. 364 as a writing activity. Write a conversation between a travel agent and customer.

☐ For additional practice, do Activity 5, p. 377 in **Más práctica gramatical.**

☐ For additional practice, do Activities 8–10, pp. 101–102 in the **Cuaderno de gramática.**

■ PRIMER PASO Self-Test

Can you talk about what you do and like to do every day?	How would you ask the following people what they do every day? 1. your best friend 2. a new student in your class 3. your cousin 4. your brother or sister 5. a group of friends 6. your teacher Look at the drawings on the **A ver si puedo...** page for this chapter (p. 382). How would you ask someone if he or she would like to do those activities?
Can you make future plans?	How do you ask someone . . . ? 1. what he or she is going to do tomorrow 2. what he or she plans to do this summer 3. what he or she hopes to do in the future Tell a friend about a future trip to Mexico. Say what you plan and hope to do. Use these cues: 1. ir a México, D. F., este verano 2. hacer turismo 3. practicar el español 4. visitar las pirámides 5. sacar fotos 6. explorar la selva

For an **online self-test,** go to **go.hrw.com.**

WV3 PUERTO RICO–12

CAPÍTULO 12

12 Las vacaciones ideales

■ SEGUNDO PASO Student Make-Up Assignments Checklist

Pupil's Edition, pp. 366–370

Study the **Vocabulario** on page 366.	☐ Do Activity 17, p. 367 as a writing activity. ☐ Do Activity 18, p. 367. ☐ For additional practice, do Activities 6–8, p. 373 in **Más práctica gramatical**. ☐ For additional practice, do Activity 12, p. 103 in the **Cuaderno de gramática**. ☐ For additional practice, do Activity 3, CD 3 in the **Interactive CD-ROM Tutor**.
Study the expressions in the **Así se dice** box on page 367: discussing what you would like to do on vacation. You should know how to find out what a friend would like to do and say what you would like to do.	☐ Do Activity 19, p. 367 as a writing activity. ☐ Do Activity 21, p. 368 as a writing activity. ☐ Do Activity 22, p. 368 as a writing activity. Write your reasons. ☐ Do Activity 23, p. 368. ☐ For additional practice, do Activities 6, 8, p. 378 in **Más práctica gramatical**.
Study the grammar presentation in the **Gramática** box on page 369: **ser** and **estar**	☐ Do Activity 24, p. 369 as a writing activity. ☐ Do Activity 25, p. 369 as a writing activity. Write the phone conversation. ☐ Do Activity 26, p. 370. ☐ Do Activity 27, p. 370 as a writing activity. Write your suggestions for places to vacation and why those places are good. ☐ Do Activity 28, p. 370 as a writing activity. ☐ For additional practice, do Activities 7–8, p. 378 in **Más práctica gramatical**. ☐ For additional practice, do Activities 13–16, pp. 104–105 in the **Cuaderno de gramática**. ☐ For additional practice, do Activity 4, CD 3 in the **Interactive CD-ROM Tutor**.

CAPÍTULO 12

■ SEGUNDO PASO Self-Test

Can you discuss what you would like to do on vacation?	How would you answer if someone asked you the following questions?
	1. ¿Qué te gustaría hacer hoy?
	2. ¿Adónde te gustaría viajar?
	How would you ask a friend on a vacation . . . ?
	1. where he or she is
	2. what it's like there
	3. what the people are like
	4. what she or he is doing right now

 For an **online self-test**, go to **go.hrw.com**.

WV3 PUERTO RICO–12

CAPÍTULO 12

12 Las vacaciones ideales

■ TERCER PASO Student Make-Up Assignments Checklist
Pupil's Edition, pp. 371–373

Study the expressions in the **Así se dice** box on page 371: saying where you went and what you did on vacation. You should know how to find out about a friend's vacation and say what you did on your vacation.	☐ For additional practice, do Activity 9, p. 379 in **Más práctica gramatical**.
	☐ For additional practice, do Activities 15–16, pp. 141–142 in the **Cuaderno de actividades**.
	☐ For additional practice, do Activity 5, CD 3 in the **Interactive CD-ROM Tutor**.
Study the grammar presentation in the **Gramática** box on page 371: the preterite tense.	☐ Do Activity 30, p. 372.
	☐ Do Activity 32, p. 373 as a writing activity.
	☐ Do Activity 33, p. 373 as a writing activity. Write about yourself.
	☐ Do Activity 34, p. 373.
	☐ For additional practice, do Activity 9, p. 379 in **Más práctica gramatical**.
	☐ For additional practice, do Activities 17–18, p. 106 in the **Cuaderno de gramática**.
	☐ For additional practice, do Activity 6, CD 3 in the **Interactive CD-ROM Tutor**.
Study the **Vocabulario** on page 372.	☐ For additional practice, do Activities 19–20, p. 107 in the **Cuaderno de gramática**.

■ TERCER PASO Self-Test

Can you say where you went and what you did on vacation?	How would you tell your friend that . . . ?

How would you tell your friend that . . . ?

1. you went to Egypt last summer

2. you and your family took a trip to Mexico City

3. you and your friends went to New York

How would you tell someone that . . . ?

1. your parents visited relatives in Chicago

2. you and your sister didn't go anywhere and worked all summer

For an **online self-test**, go to **go.hrw.com**.

WV3 PUERTO RICO–12

CAPÍTULO 12

Quizzes

Nombre _____ Clase _____ Fecha _____

¡Mucho gusto!

■ PRIMER PASO

Grammar and Vocabulary

A. Nine of the items on Danny's spelling quiz are missing accents, tildes, or punctuation marks. Write the correct form of each word or expression below. (9 points)

1. Buenos dias.   _____

2. manana   _____

3. Adios.   _____

4. Mucho gusto!   _____

5. ¿Como te llamas?   _____

6. Qué tal?   _____

7. Este es mi amigo.   _____

8. senora   _____

9. ¿Y tu?   _____

SCORE [   ]

B. Indicate the subject of each statement or question by writing **yo** or **tú** next to each. (7 points)

_____ 10. ¿Te llamas Lucía?

_____ 11. Tengo que irme.

_____ 12. ¿Cómo estás hoy?

_____ 13. Estoy bien, gracias.

_____ 14. ¿Cómo te llamas?

_____ 15. Bueno, tengo clase.

_____ 16. Me llamo Paloma.

SCORE [   ]

Alternative Quiz 1-1A

CAPÍTULO 1

C. Match each question or statement in the column on the left with the most appropriate response from the right-hand column. (10 points)

_____ 17. Adiós, señora Rodríguez.

_____ 18. ¿Cómo te llamas?

_____ 19. ¡Buenos días, don Gregorio!

_____ 20. ¿Cómo estás hoy?

_____ 21. Encantado.

a. Me llamo Pilar.
b. Estoy bien, gracias.
c. Igualmente.
d. Hola, Juana María.
e. Hasta mañana, Diego.

SCORE _____

D. Complete the conversation between Isabel and Ignacio with the expressions from the box. (9 points)

| Tengo que irme | Más o menos | me llamo | Encantada | Estupenda |
| qué tal | Igualmente | Hasta luego | estás | |

ISABEL   ¡Hola! ¿Cómo te llamas?

IGNACIO   Hola, _____ Ignacio Soza. ¿Y tú?
                                    22.

ISABEL   Soy Isabel Huerta. _____.
                                        23.

IGNACIO   _____. ¿Cómo _____ hoy, Isabel?
                    24.   25.

ISABEL   _____, gracias. ¿Y tú, ¿ _____?
                    26.   27.

IGNACIO   _____. Tengo clase ahora.
                    28.

            _____.
                    29.

ISABEL   Bueno, Ignacio. _____.
                                        30.

SCORE _____

TOTAL SCORE _____ /35

Nombre _____ Clase _____ Fecha _____

¡Mucho gusto!

■ SEGUNDO PASO

Grammar and Vocabulary

A. Ask and explain where new classmates are from, using the correct form of the verb **ser.** (10 points)

1. Teresa _____ de Miami.

2. Jorge _____ de México.

3. ¿Tú _____ de California?

4. Mi amiga Delia _____ de San Antonio.

5. Yo _____ de Chicago.

SCORE _____

B. Complete everyone's questions with the correct question words. (5 points)

6. Hola, Benjamín, ¿_____ estás?

7. Carlota, ¿de _____ eres?

8. Hola, soy Toña. ¿_____ te llamas?

9. Nacho, ¿_____ años tienes?

10. Hola, Leonardo, ¿_____ tal?

SCORE _____

Alternative Quiz 1-2A

C. Write out these math problems and solve them, spelling all numbers as words. (10 points)

11. _____ + _____ = _____
          18   7

12. _____ + _____ = _____
          13   9

13. _____ + _____ = _____
          8   12

14. _____ + _____ = _____
          20   3

15. _____ + _____ = _____
          12   6

SCORE [   ]

D. Leonor is telling you the phone numbers of some classmates. Write out the phone numbers in numerals. (5 points)

16. El número de Verónica es el cuatro cinco nueve, veinticuatro treinta. _____

17. El número de Maricarmen es el dos tres cinco, once veintiséis. _____

18. El número de Juan Carlos es el siete nueve uno, trece catorce. _____

19. El número de Luciano es el ocho cuatro seis, quince veintisiete. _____

20. El número de Inés es el tres seis siete, doce dieciséis. _____

SCORE [   ]

TOTAL SCORE [   ] /30

Nombre _____ Clase _____ Fecha _____

1 ¡Mucho gusto!

■ TERCER PASO

Grammar and Vocabulary

A. Complete the lists below with the Spanish words that belong in each category. Include definite articles in your answers. (15 points)

tipos de *(types of)* música

1. _____

2. _____

deportes

5. _____

6. _____

7. _____

8. _____

clases

3. _____

4. _____

comida

9. _____

10. _____

SCORE ☐

B. You are talking with Fernando, the new student. In Spanish, ask him if he likes . . . (8 points)

11. the cafeteria _____

_____

12. English class _____

_____

Now explain to Fernando that . . .

13. you like Italian food, but you like Chinese food more. _____

_____

14. you don't like homework. _____

_____

SCORE ☐

CAPÍTULO 1

Alternative Quiz 1-3A

C. Dora and Alberto are talking about sports. Complete their conversation with the missing words from the box. (12 points)

gusta	no	te	más
Qué	mucho	me	pero

ALBERTO   Dora, ¿ _____ gusta el baloncesto?
                                    15.

DORA   Sí, _____ gusta, _____ me gusta más el béisbol.
                      16.   17.

ALBERTO   ¡Uf! El béisbol _____ me gusta. ¡Es horrible!
                                      18.

DORA   ¿ _____ te gusta?
                  19.

ALBERTO   Pues, me gusta _____ el tenis.
                                        20.

DORA   ¿Y la natación?

ALBERTO   Sí, me _____, pero me gusta _____ el tenis.
                          21.   22.

SCORE [   ]

TOTAL SCORE [   ] /35

CAPÍTULO 2

¡Organízate!

PRIMER PASO

Maximum Score: 35

Grammar and Vocabulary

A. Complete these statements about what different people need and want to buy at the book-store with the correct subject pronoun: **yo, tú, él,** or **ella.** (8 points)

1. Toña, ¿_____ necesitas papel?

2. _____ quiero muchas cosas.

3. _____ necesito un diccionario para la clase de español.

4. ¿Qué quiere tu amiga Celia? ¿_____ quiere una mochila?

5. ¿Y Francisco? ¿Qué necesita _____?

6. ¿Qué necesita la profesora? _____ necesita más libros.

7. ¿_____ quieres un diccionario de español o un diccionario de inglés?

8. ¿Y el señor Hurtado? _____ quiere una calculadora.

SCORE _____

B. You found several of each of the things below when cleaning out your backpack and desk. Write the plural form of each noun with its correct indefinite article. (12 points)

9. carpeta _____

10. papel _____

11. goma _____

12. libro _____

13. lápiz _____

14. cuaderno _____

SCORE _____

CAPÍTULO 2

Alternative Quiz 2-1A

C. What does everyone need to buy? Complete the sentences with the correct indefinite article. (8 points)

15. ¿Necesitas _____ mochila o _____ carpeta?

16. Necesito _____ calculadora y _____ cuaderno.

17. Mariana necesita _____ diccionario y _____ regla.

18. Mi amigo necesita _____ goma de borrar y _____ lápiz.

SCORE _____

D. Your friend wants to learn some Spanish. Tell him the Spanish words for the things he needs to . . . (7 points)

19. multiply and divide _____

20. carry books and school supplies _____

21. find out how to spell a word _____

22. write in ink _____

23. hold loose papers _____

24. write an essay or do his homework on _____

25. draw a straight line _____

SCORE _____

TOTAL SCORE _____ /35

CAPÍTULO 2

¡Organízate!

SEGUNDO PASO

Grammar and Vocabulary

A. Complete the questions and statements about what people have and need with the correct forms of **cuánto** and **mucho**. Remember to make these adjectives match the nouns they describe. (14 points)

1. ¿_____ sillas hay en la cafetería?

2. ¿_____ papeles tienes en tu mochila?

3. ¿_____ revistas quieres?

4. ¿Tienes _____ carteles en tu cuarto?

5. No tengo _____ lámparas en mi cuarto.

6. Hay _____ libros en la clase.

7. Necesito _____ ropa para el colegio.

SCORE [   ]

B. Complete Carmelo's description of his room with the missing Spanish equivalents of the English words in parentheses. (9 points)

¿Cómo es mi _____? Pues, tengo _____ y
        8. *(room)*   **9.** *(a bed)*

_____. También tengo _____ y _____.
  10. *(a closet)*   **11.** *(a radio)*   **12.** *(some posters)*

Y hay dos _____ y _____. Tengo _____
      13. *(windows)*   **14.** *(a door)*   **15.** *(a chair)*

y _____ también.
  16. *(a lamp)*

SCORE [   ]

Alternative Quiz 2-2A

C. Explain how many of each item are left in the department store after the sale. Use **hay** and the inventory chart below. Write all numbers as words. (12 points)

relojes	18
armarios	25
escritorios	21
camas	12
televisores	15
mesas	30

17. _____

18. _____

19. _____

20. _____

21. _____

22. _____

SCORE [   ]

TOTAL SCORE [   ] /35

CAPÍTULO 2

2 ¡Organízate!

CAPÍTULO

TERCER PASO

Grammar and Vocabulary

A. Explain to Alejandro how much money he needs to buy the following things. Write out all numbers. (8 points)

1. un televisor/$199.00   _____

2. un escritorio/$121.00   _____

3. tres carteles/$38.00   _____

4. un diccionario español-inglés/47.00   _____

5. una silla/$64.00   _____

6. unas zapatillas de tenis/$76.00   _____

7. un armario/$165.00   _____

8. un radio/$53.00   _____

SCORE [   ]

B. Read the sentences, then indicate what each person needs to do for that situation or problem. (8 points)

_____ 9. Andrés has books, papers, and CDs all over his room.

_____ 10. Claudia wants some new clothes for school.

_____ 11. Ernesto needs school supplies, a watch, and some new sneakers.

_____ 12. Lucía has three assignments due tomorrow.

_____ 13. Darío's clothes are all over his bedroom floor.

_____ 14. Pamela is a new student, and doesn't know anyone.

_____ 15. Toño is really hungry.

_____ 16. Marcia can't find the money her mom gave her in her purse.

a. organizar el cuarto
b. encontrar el dinero
c. hacer la tarea
d. ir al centro comercial
e. poner la ropa en el armario
f. ir a la pizzería
g. comprar muchas cosas
h. conocer a muchos amigos nuevos

SCORE [   ]

CAPÍTULO 2

Alternative Quiz 2-3A

C. Verónica and Rafael are talking after school. Complete their conversation with the missing words from the box. (9 points)

quieres	hacer la tarea	Quiero	ir a la pizzería	organizar
necesitas		poner	encontrar	comprar muchas cosas

VERÓNICA Rafael, ¿qué quieres hacer?

RAFAEL 17. _____ ir al centro comercial. Necesito

18. _____.

VERÓNICA ¿Qué cosas 19. _____ comprar?

RAFAEL Muchas cosas para mis clases y mi cuarto. ¿Y qué 20. _____

hacer tú?

VERÓNICA Pues, yo quiero 21. _____. Me gusta mucho la pizza. Pero nece-

sito 22. _____ mi dinero primero.

RAFAEL ¿Tienes mucha tarea? ¿Quieres 23. _____ después

(afterwards)?

VERÓNICA Sí, buena idea. Pero antes *(before)*, necesito 24. _____ mi

cuarto.

RAFAEL Yo también. Necesito 25. _____ mucha ropa en el armario.

SCORE [____]

D. Complete the statements by writing out the numbers in parentheses as words. (5 points)

26. Necesito _____ (81) dólares para comprar unas zapatillas de tenis.

27. Hay _____ (31) mesas en la cafetería.

28. Toño tiene _____ (67) centavos *(cents)* en su mochila.

29. Hay _____ (21) estudiantes en mi clase de español.

30. Hay _____ (25) revistas en el cuarto de Carlos.

SCORE [____]   TOTAL SCORE [____] /30

CAPÍTULO 3

Nuevas clases, nuevos amigos

■ PRIMER PASO

Grammar and Vocabulary

A. Read what class Ernestina has right now, and then write a sentence explaining what time it is. Use the information in Ernestina's schedule. (12 points)

Hora	Clase
8:00	Química
8:55	Computación
9:40	Geografía
10:05	Ciencias sociales
10:45	Francés
11:30	Descanso
12:50	Inglés
13:25	Educación física

1. Tiene francés ahora. _____

_____

2. Ahora tiene la clase de computación. _____

_____

3. Necesita ir a la clase de educación física ahora.

_____

_____

4. Su clase de geografía es ahora. _____

5. Tiene inglés ahora. _____

6. Ahora tiene la clase de química. _____

SCORE [   ]

B. Complete the sentences about what classes people have this afternoon with the missing Spanish words. (8 points)

7. Andrea tiene _____ *(English)* y _____ *(art)*.

8. Mi amigo Miguel Ángel tiene _____ *(geography)* y

_____ *(social sciences)*.

9. Tengo _____ *(computer science)*.

10. ¿Tienes _____ *(math)* también?

11. Yadira tiene _____ *(science)* y _____ *(physical

education)*.

SCORE [   ]

CAPÍTULO 3

Alternative Quiz 3-1A

C. Daniela is running late, and her mom is helping her get ready for school. Complete their conversation with the correct definite articles. (15 points)

MAMÁ   Daniela, es tarde. Ya son las ocho. ¿Tienes _____ mochila y
                                                                   12.

_____ libros?
        13.

DANIELA   Sí, mamá. Pero... ¿dónde están _____ carpetas para
                                                    14.

_____ clases de inglés y francés?
            15.

MAMÁ   Están aquí, en la mesa. ¿Y qué más necesitas? ¿ _____ cuader-
                                                                16.

nos? ¿ _____ zapatillas de tenis?
         17.

DANIELA   Sí, y también necesito _____ tarea y
                                            18.

_____ almuerzo.
        19.

MAMÁ   Bien. ¿Tienes _____ carteles para tu clase de arte?
                            20.

DANIELA   Sí. Y también necesito _____ revistas para mi clase de inglés.
                                            21.

SCORE ☐

TOTAL SCORE ☐ /35

CAPÍTULO 3

CAPÍTULO 3

Nuevas clases, nuevos amigos

■ SEGUNDO PASO

Maximum Score: 30

Grammar and Vocabulary

A. Everyone brought in props for the class play, and now they're all mixed up. Explain to whom each prop belongs, using the list below. (6 points)

1.	**televisor**	el profesor Ibarra
2.	**libro de francés**	Sonia
3.	**reloj**	la profesora Cortez
4.	**zapatillas de tenis**	el director Muñoz
5.	**ropa**	el estudiante nuevo
6.	**calculadora**	Ricardo

1. _____

2. _____

3. _____

4. _____

5. _____

6. _____

SCORE _____

B. Write a sentence explaining at what time the classes and events below take place, using the cues given. Spell out all numbers as words. (12 points)

7. la clase de computación (8:20 a.m.) _____

8. la clase de inglés (12:30 p.m.) _____

9. el almuerzo (1:00 p.m.) _____

10. el descanso (2:50 p.m.) _____

11. el programa de televisión (5:30 p.m.) _____

12. la fiesta (9:15 p.m) _____

CAPÍTULO 3

Alternative Quiz 3-2A

13. el concierto de jazz (7:45 p.m.) _____

14. la clase de matemáticas (10:10 a.m.) _____

SCORE [   ]

C. Explain at what time you want or need to do the following activities. Begin your sentences with **Necesito…** or **Quiero…** and mention a different time for each activity. Remember to explain if the activity will take place in the morning, afternoon, or evening. (12 points)

15. ir al centro comercial _____

16. poner la ropa en el armario _____

17. ir a la clase de español _____

18. ir a la pizzería con amigos _____

19. hacer la tarea _____

20. organizar tu cuarto _____

SCORE [   ]

TOTAL SCORE [   ] /30

CAPÍTULO 3

Nuevas clases, nuevos amigos

■ TERCER PASO

Maximum Score: 35

Grammar and Vocabulary

A. Read what you and some classmates want to do this weekend. Then explain what each person likes, using the words in the box below and the correct form of **gustar.** (7.5 points)

las novelas	*los deportes*	*las fiestas*	*los conciertos*	*los videojuegos*

1. Alejandra quiere jugar *(to play)* al voleibol y al tenis.

   _____

2. Tú quieres ir al concierto, ¿verdad?

   _____

3. Toño quiere comprar un videojuego nuevo.

   _____

4. Rodrigo quiere ir a una fiesta.

   _____

5. Yo quiero ir a la librería.

   _____

SCORE [   ]

B. You want to find out more about the new student Rosaura. Ask your friend if she likes the following things. Use tag questions and the correct form of **gustar.** (7.5 points)

6. el colegio _____

7. los partidos _____

8. los bailes _____

9. las fiestas _____

10. la comida china _____

SCORE [   ]

C A P Í T U L O 3

Alternative Quiz 3-3A

C. Disagree with everything your friends say by writing the opposite of their opinions. Remember to use the correct form of the adjective. (12 points)

11. La directora es antipática. _____

12. El colegio es grande. _____

13. La tarea es fácil. _____

14. La cafetería es fea. _____

15. Los estudiantes son aburridos. _____

16. Las clases son malas. _____

17. La profesora es baja. _____

18. El profesor es rubio. _____

SCORE ☐

D. Below are a series of descriptions of some of the people and things at school. Match each subject with its correct description. (8 points)

_____ 19. Es grande, nuevo y bonito.

_____ 20. Es aburrida y difícil.

_____ 21. Son inteligentes y simpáticas.

_____ 22. Es nueva y pequeña.

_____ 23. Son muy bonitos.

_____ 24. Es estricto pero interesante.

_____ 25. Son muy cómicos.

_____ 26. Es muy mala.

a. Mónica y Marta
b. el profesor
c. la tarea
d. mis amigos
e. el colegio
f. la radio
g. la comida de la cafetería
h. los carteles

SCORE ☐

TOTAL SCORE ☐ /35

Spanish 1 ¡Ven conmigo!, Chapter 3

CAPÍTULO 3

¿Qué haces esta tarde?

■ PRIMER PASO

Grammar and Vocabulary

A. Clara is explaining how she and her family spend a typical Saturday. Complete her description with the correct form of the missing verbs. Each verb will be used only once. (15 points)

descansar	preparar	cuidar	tomar	hablar
hacer	mirar	pasar	lavar	caminar

Por la mañana, organizo mi cuarto. Mamá **1.** _____ a mi hermanito

Eduardo. Luego, ella y yo **2.** _____ con el perro en el parque. Arturo y papá

3. _____ el coche. A veces papá **4.** _____ un partido de fút-

bol en la televisión. También él **5.** _____ el rato con sus amigos en el café.

Más tarde, Arturo y yo **6.** _____ la cena y mamá **7.** _____

en su cuarto. Después de cenar, yo **8.** _____ un helado con mis amigas, o

9. _____ por teléfono. ¿Y tú? ¿Qué **10.** _____ en el tiempo libre?

SCORE _____

B. Discuss what you and your friends like to do in your free time. Using the drawings, write a sentence or question with the correct form of **gustar.** (10 points)

11. Juan Antonio	12. Antonieta	13. yo	14. Marcelina	15. tú

11. _____

12. _____

13. _____

14. _____

15. ¿_____?

SCORE _____

Alternative Quiz 4-1 A

C. Explain to your new neighbor Ricardo who the different members of the Mora family are. Use the word **que** to connect the two parts of your sentences, and use a different verb in each sentence. (5 points)

MODELO   La persona que escucha música es Sonia.

16. Lucía   17. doña Dora

18. don Francisco   19. Toño

20. Sonia

16. _____

17. _____

18. _____

19. _____

20. _____

SCORE ⬜

D. Complete the sentences about who does free-time activities together with **con** and the correct pronoun. Remember that *with me* and *with you* have special forms. (5 points)

21. Por la tarde, papá prepara la cena. Necesito preparar la cena _____ .

22. Después de clases, Mariana necesita ir al centro comercial. Quiero ir _____ .

23. Me gusta hablar por teléfono, y a Javier le gusta también. Él habla _____ mucho.

24. Montas en bicicleta hoy, ¿verdad? ¿Quién monta en bicicleta _____ ?

25. Por la tarde, Azucena trabaja en un restaurante. Yo trabajo _____ .

SCORE ⬜

TOTAL SCORE ⬜ /35

Nombre _____ Clase _____ Fecha _____

¿Qué haces esta tarde?

■ SEGUNDO PASO

Maximum Score: 35

Grammar and Vocabulary

A. Angélica calls her friend Esmeralda after school. Complete their conversation with the correct forms of the verb **estar.** (12 points)

ANGÉLICA   Hola, Esmeralda. Soy yo, Angélica.

ESMERALDA   Angélica, hola. ¿Qué tal? ¿**1.** _____ en casa ahora?

ANGÉLICA   No, **2.** _____ en el centro, con Sara y Raúl. Nosotros

            3. _____ en la pizzería.

ESMERALDA   **4.** _____ Uds. en la pizzería al lado del parque?

ANGÉLICA   No, en la pizzería que **5.** _____ al lado del gimnasio. Oye,

            ¿quieres ir con nosotros ahora a tomar un helado?

ESMERALDA   Sí, quiero ir, pero es imposible. Ahora yo **6.** _____ en casa con

            mi hermanito. Oye, Angélica, ¿**7.** _____ Lucía allí con Uds.?

ANGÉLICA   No, ella y Toño **8.** _____ en la plaza.

SCORE [_____]

B. Read what different people are doing, then write a sentence explaining what place each person or group is in right now. Use subject pronouns, the correct form of **estar,** and a different place in each sentence. (14 points)

restaurante	biblioteca	piscina	supermercado	casa	gimnasio	tienda

9. Nora y sus amigas nadan.

    _____.

10. Lavo los platos y después saco la basura.

    _____.

11. Ernesto compra comida para la cena.

    _____.

Alternative Quiz 4-2A

12. Joaquín sirve *(serves)* comida mexicana a muchas personas.

_____.

13. Tú y Tatiana practican el baloncesto.

_____.

14. Anabel y Juan Pablo estudian para un examen.

_____.

15. David y yo compramos ropa.

_____.

SCORE ☐

C. Answer the questions about what everyone does after school. Use subject pronouns and the correct form of the infinitives given in your answers. (9 points)

16. ¿Y tú? (trabajar en un restaurante)

_____

17. ¿Y tú y Marta Inés? (pasar el rato con amigos)

_____

18. ¿Qué hace José Antonio después de clases? (tocar la guitarra)

_____

19. ¿Y la profesora? (escuchar música)

_____

20. ¿Y Juan José y Marcelo? (mirar la televisión)

_____

21. ¿Y Mila y Sofía? (bailar con un grupo de baile)

_____

SCORE ☐

TOTAL SCORE ☐ /35

4 ¿Qué haces esta tarde?

Alternative Quiz 4-3A

Maximum Score: 30

■ TERCER PASO

Grammar and Vocabulary

A. Your friend is writing a letter to a pen pal in Mexico about her schedule, and needs your help with some sentences. Write the Spanish equivalents for the missing words. (9 points)

1. _____, necesito cuidar a mi hermanita.
   On Thursdays

2. _____, voy a un restaurante con mi familia.
   On Saturday

3. _____, siempre descanso.
   On the weekends

4. _____, tengo un examen de inglés.
   On Monday

5. _____, voy a mi clase de francés.
   On Tuesdays

6. _____, quiero ir al parque.
   On Friday

SCORE [   ]

B. Complete Yadira's note to her friend with the correct form of the verb **ir.** (9 points)

¿Qué haces esta tarde? Yo tengo mucha tarea, y primero _____ a casa para
                                                              7.

estudiar. Después quiero _____ al café para tomar un refresco. Tú
                              8.

_____ conmigo, ¿verdad? Antonieta no _____ porque tiene
       9.   10.

clase de arte. Pero mañana ella y yo _____ al cine. Tú y Juan José
                                          11.

_____ también, ¿no?
      12.

SCORE [   ]

CAPÍTULO 4

Alternative Quiz 4-3A

C. Use the correct form of **ir** and **para** + *infinitive* to explain where everyone is going today, and what they are going to do at those places. For each place, choose a different, logical infinitive from the list. (12 points)

MODELO   Félix/casa
Félix va a casa para descansar.

| estudiar   montar en bicicleta   tomar un refresco   comprar comida |
| ver una película   tomar una clase de baile   comprar ropa   nadar |

13. tú y Francisca/gimnasio _____

14. mis amigos/tienda _____

15. yo/parque _____

16. Víctor/piscina _____

17. Papá/supermercado _____

18. tú/biblioteca _____

19. mis amigos y yo/café _____

20. Beatriz y Marcela/cine _____

SCORE [   ]

TOTAL SCORE [/30]

Spanish 1 ¡Ven conmigo!, Chapter 4

CAPÍTULO **5**

El ritmo de la vida

■ PRIMER PASO

Grammar and Vocabulary

A. Complete María Teresa's questions about who's doing what after school today with **quién** or **quiénes.** (5 points)

1. ¿_____ trabajan o van a la bibioteca?

2. ¿_____ quiere ir al parque conmigo?

3. ¿_____ practican el voleibol con Víctor?

4. ¿_____ va al café?

5. ¿Con _____ habla por teléfono Lourdes? ¿Habla con Marta?

SCORE [   ]

B. Andrea is interviewing her classmate Rogelio about his daily routine. Complete their conversation with the missing expressions from the box. Use a different expression for each blank. (8 points)

todavía	muchas veces		siempre		durante la semana
sólo cuando		todos los días		con qué frecuencia	a veces

ANDREA   Rogelio, ¿cómo es una semana típica para ti?

ROGELIO   Pues, **6.** _____ hago muchas cosas. Voy a clase, al trabajo

y al gimnasio.

ANDREA   ¿Y **7.** _____ vas al gimnasio? ¿Un día, dos días, tres días...?

ROGELIO   Voy allí **8.** _____ después de clases, y los fines de semana

también. Me gusta mucho ir al gimnasio.

ANDREA   ¿Y **9.** _____ vas con tus amigos?

ROGELIO   No siempre, pero sí **10.** _____ mis amigos van conmigo para jugar

al baloncesto.

ANDREA   ¿Y **11.** _____ nadas en la piscina también?

ROGELIO   Sí, me gusta nadar, pero **12.** _____ tengo tiempo.

C A P Í T U L O 5

Alternative Quiz 5-1A

ANDREA ¿Y 13. _____ trabajas todas las noches?

ROGELIO No, ahora trabajo sólo los lunes y los jueves.

C. Answer the questions about Ramona and her daily routine, using negative words such as **no**, **nadie**, **nada**, and **nunca**. (9 points)

14. ¿Con quién va Ramona al centro comercial? _____

15. ¿Cuándo cuida a su hermanita? _____

16. ¿Qué quiere comprar Ramona para su cuarto? _____

17. ¿Quién camina con ella en el parque? _____

18. ¿Siempre estudia ella los fines de semana? _____

19. ¿Qué necesita comprar Julia para las clases? _____

SCORE

D. Juan José leads a very boring life. Complete his description of a typical week with the correct missing negative words: **no, nadie, nada, nunca.** Some of the words may be used more than once. (8 points)

_____ hago _____ durante la semana.
20. 21.

Después de clases, _____ voy al parque con mis amigos. Voy a
22.

casa, pero _____ miro la televisión. Sólo hago la tarea, pero
23.

_____ estudia conmigo. _____ hablo por teléfono. Los fines
24. 25.

de semana también son muy aburridos. A veces voy al gimnasio o al cine, pero

_____ voy con _____.
26. 27.

SCORE

TOTAL SCORE /30

CAPÍTULO 5

Nombre _____ Clase _____ Fecha _____

5 El ritmo de la vida

■ SEGUNDO PASO

Grammar and Vocabulary

A. Complete the conversations about what everyone does using the correct form of the verbs in parentheses. (13 points)

—¿Qué _____ Iván en la biblioteca? ¿ _____ la tarea él y Diego?
    1. (hacer)   **2. (Hacer)**

—No, ellos no estudian ahora. _____ revistas y
                                3. (Leer)

_____ cartas a sus amigos.
4. (escribir)

—Claudia, ¿tú y Luz _____ ejercicio juntas?
                        5. (hacer)

—Sí, yo _____ ejercicio con ella todos los días. Muchas veces ella y yo
         6. (hacer)

_____ en el parque. A veces _____ a una clase de ejercicios
   7. (correr)   **8. (asistir)**

aeróbicos también.

—Ignacio, ¿qué _____ ustedes en la cafetería del colegio?
                  9. (comer)

—Yo _____ un sándwich y _____ jugo. Mi amigo Cristóbal
     10. (comer)   **11. (beber)**

_____ pizza y ensaladas y _____ agua.
   12. (comer)   **13. (beber)**

SCORE [   ]

Alternative Quiz 5-2A

B. Clara is wondering what to get people for birthday presents. Answer her questions by telling her what each person or group likes to do. Use the infinitives given with **gusta** and the correct pronoun. Include the phrases **a él, a ella, a ellos,** or **a ellas** for clarification. (10 points)

14. ¿Qué hacen José Ángel y Salvador? (asistir al teatro)

_____

15. ¿Qué hace Anabel? (correr)

_____

16. ¿Qué hacen Pilar y Gregorio? (jugar al tenis)

_____

17. ¿Qué hace Jaime? (bucear)

_____

18. ¿Qué hacen Rosario y Graciela? (acampar)

_____

SCORE [   ]

C. Complete the statements about where people go and what activities they like to do in each place. Write the missing pronouns and then choose most logical infinitive from the box. Use each infinitive only once. (12 points)

> hacer ejercicio   recibir
> comer   esquiar   leer   pescar

19. Ricardo y yo vamos al restaurante porque _____ gusta _____ hamburguesas.

20. Julia y Sara van a Colorado porque _____ gusta _____ .

21. Abel y Roberto van al lago porque _____ gusta _____ .

22. Yo escribo muchas cartas porque _____ gusta _____ cartas también.

23. Yvón va a la librería porque _____ gusta _____ todas las revistas nuevas.

24. A ustedes _____ gusta _____ en el gimnasio nuevo, ¿verdad?

SCORE [   ]

TOTAL SCORE [   ] /35

CAPÍTULO 5

El ritmo de la vida

Alternative Quiz 5-3A

Maximum Score: 35

■ TERCER PASO

Grammar and Vocabulary

A. Write the Spanish words that correspond to the definitions. (9 points)

1. El primer mes de la primavera es _____.

2. El mes después de abril es _____.

3. El mes antes de octubre es _____.

4. El primer mes del año es _____.

5. La estación después del otoño es _____.

6. El mes después de julio es _____.

7. Hay doce _____ en un año.

8. Tres meses forman una _____.

9. La estación antes del verano es _____.

SCORE [   ]

B. Marisol wants to know what's going to be happening in the next few weeks. Answer her questions about when events take place, writing complete sentences and using the information given. (14 points)

○	October		November	
game		15th	dance	1st
test		21th	concert	5th
○ party		27th	dinner	22nd
trip to park		31th		

10. ¿Cuándo es el examen? _____

11. ¿Cuándo es la excursión *(trip)* al parque? _____

12. ¿Cuándo es la fiesta? _____

13. ¿Cuándo es el concierto? _____

Alternative Quiz 5-3A

14. ¿Cuándo es el partido? _____

15. ¿Cuándo es la cena en tu casa? _____

16. ¿Cuándo es el baile? _____

SCORE [   ]

C. Write a sentence in Spanish describing the weather in each place listed. Explain whether it's hot, cold, or cool, and what the other conditions are in each place. Use the information in the chart. (12 points)

Ciudad	Temperatura máxima	Temperatura mínima	Tiempo
Nueva York	60°	45°	
Miami	100°	85°	
Chicago	45°	40°	
San Francisco	65°	55°	
Juneau	35°	25°	
San Antonio	85°	70°	

17. _____

18. _____

19. _____

20. _____

21. _____

22. _____

SCORE [   ]

TOTAL SCORE [   ] /35

CAPÍTULO 5

CAPÍTULO 6

Entre familia

Alternative Quiz 6-1 A

Maximum Score: 35

■ PRIMER PASO

Grammar and Vocabulary

A. Ricky is writing a description of his family for Spanish class and needs your help. Complete these sentences with the missing Spanish words. (16 points)

1. _____ están divorciados. **2.** Mis hermanos y yo vivimos con
(*My parents*)

_____. **3.** Marisol, la nueva esposa de mi papá, es
(*our mother*)

_____. **4.** _____ son Tomás y Sergio. **5.** Ellos son
(*my stepmother*)   (*Her children*)

_____. **6.** _____ vive en Chicago.
(*my stepbrothers*)   (*Their father*)

7. _____ viven en Chicago también. **8.** _____ se
(*Their cousins*)   (*Our dogs*)

llaman Capitán y Oso.

SCORE [   ]

B. Look at the Gómez family tree, then complete the statements with the missing words. (10 points)

8. Fernanda es la _____ de Luis.

9. Geraldo es el _____ de Fabiola.

10. Luis y Pascual son _____.

11. Clara es la _____ de Fabiola.

12. La _____ de Pedro es María.

13. La _____ de María es Clara.

14. Pascual es el _____ de Fernanda.

15. María es la _____ de Geraldo.

16. Diego es el _____ de Elisa.

17. Elisa es la _____ de Luis.

Diego   **Clara**

Geraldo   **María**   **Pedro**   **Fernanda**

Luis   **Fabiola**   **Pascual**   **Elisa**

SCORE [   ]

CAPÍTULO 6

Alternative Quiz 6-1A

C. Look over the family tree again, then read what different members of his family say about one another. Put a check mark next to the person most likely to have made each statement.
(9 points)

18. Mis hijos y mi esposa son morenos, pero soy rubio.

_____ Geraldo

_____ Clara

_____ Fernanda

19. Qué similares son mi esposa y mi hija, ¿verdad? Las dos son altas y rubias.

_____ Diego

_____ Pedro

_____ Geraldo

20. Mi hijo sólo tiene 12 años, pero es muy alto. Es moreno, como su tío.

_____ Pedro

_____ Diego

_____ María

21. No me gusta mi prima Fabiola. Es muy antipática.

_____ María

_____ Elisa

_____ Luis

22. ¡Qué buena es la hija de mi hijo Pedro! Estudia mucho y es muy inteligente.

_____ Clara

_____ Fernanda

_____ María

23. Me gusta visitar a mis abuelos. Mi abuelo es estricto pero simpático.

_____ Pascual

_____ Fernanda

_____ Clara

SCORE _____

TOTAL SCORE _____ /35

CAPÍTULO 6

Entre familia

■ SEGUNDO PASO

Grammar and Vocabulary

A. Salvador and Manuel are talking about their families. Complete their conversation with the words and expressions from the box. Use each expression only once. (12 points)

| viejos | travieso | menor | De qué color es | canas | pelirrojo |
| ojos | | se ve | mayor | atractiva | cómo son | listos |

SALVADOR   Manuel, ¿**1.** _____ tus hermanos?

MANUEL   Son muy **2.** _____. Toño, mi hermano

3. _____, tiene 17 años. Gerardo, mi hermano

4. _____, tiene 10 años. Es muy **5.** _____.

SALVADOR   ¿Ellos son rubios, como tú? ¿**6.** _____ el pelo de Toño?

MANUEL   Toño es **7.** _____, como mi mamá. Pero Gerardo sí es rubio,

como yo. Y los dos tienen **8.** _____ verdes.

SALVADOR   ¿Y cuántos años tienen tus abuelos? ¿Son muy **9.** _____?

MANUEL   Pues, mi abuelo tiene 68 años. Él tiene **10.** _____ y es un poco

gordo. Y mi abuela tiene 60 años. Ella todavía **11.** _____ joven.

Es una mujer muy **12.** _____.

SCORE _____

B. There are a lot of similarities between different members of the Chávez family. Complete the statements about how different relatives resemble one another with the correct form of the adjectives. (8 points)

13. ¡Qué travieso es Roberto! Sus hermanas también son muy _____.

14. Francisco es muy alto y delgado, porque sus padres son _____ y _____.

15. La tía Anabel es pelirroja, y sus hijos son _____ también.

16. El abuelo es un poco gordo, y su hija Andrea también es un poco _____.

17. Julieta es muy lista, y sus tres hermanos son _____ también. Es una familia muy inteligente.

Alternative Quiz 6-2A

18. El abuelo se ve muy joven, ¿verdad? Y los tíos también se ven muy _____ para su edad.

19. La abuela tiene 70 años, pero es una mujer muy atractiva. Sus hermanas también son muy _____.

SCORE [   ]

C. Read the statements about what the Peña family is doing this weekend, and complete each one with the personal **a** if necessary. If it's not necessary, mark an X in the blank. (6 points)

20. La señora Peña quiere ir al centro y mirar _____ unas tiendas.

21. Luisa va a una fiesta en casa de su amiga Anaís. Quiere conocer _____ toda su familia.

22. María del Carmen y Julio van al cine para ver _____ la película nueva.

23. La abuela quiere ir al parque y ver _____ todas las personas que están allí.

24. El señor Peña necesita ir al hospital para visitar _____ un amigo que está allí.

25. A Heriberto le gusta el arte. Quiere ver _____ las nuevas pinturas *(paintings)* en el museo de arte.

SCORE [   ]

D. Complete Claudia's description of what she and her family do on weekends with the correct form of **hacer** or **salir.** (9 points)

¿Qué _____ mi familia y yo los fines de semana? Pues, los sábados, ayudo mucho
       26.

en casa. Por la mañana siempre _____ las camas. Pero mi hermano nunca
                                  27.

_____ nada. ¡Él es muy perezoso! El sábado por la noche, todos nosotros _____
28.   29.

juntos para cenar en mi restaurante favorito. El domingo, yo _____ con mis amigas.
                                                               30.

Muchas veces vamos al parque. Mis padres también _____. Van a la casa de mis tíos.
                                                    31.

SCORE [   ]

TOTAL SCORE [/35]

Spanish 1 ¡Ven conmigo!, Chapter 6

6 Entre familia

■ TERCER PASO

Maximum Score: 30

Grammar and Vocabulary

A. Paco's family just found out that Aunt Cleotilda is coming over for a surprise visit. Complete what Paco says about getting the house cleaned up with the correct form of **poner.** (6 points)

1. Mamá _____ la ropa en el armario.

2. Yo _____ todos mis libros y revistas en el escritorio.

3. Papá y Juan Alberto _____ la mesa.

4. Sara _____ su mochila en su cuarto.

5. Mamá, ¿dónde _____ nosotros la aspiradora? ¿Debajo de la cama?

6. Federico necesita _____ sus zapatillas en su cuarto.

SCORE [ ]

B. El señor Ramos has some ideas about what his family should do. Complete what he says to his wife Inés with the correct form of **deber.** (8 points)

Inés, estoy un poco gordo. **7.** _____ ir al gimnasio para hacer ejercicio

todos los días. Y tú, mi amor, trabajas demasiado. **8.** _____ descansar más.

Tengo una idea. Todos nosotros **9.** _____ ayudar más en casa con los

quehaceres. Pepe y Luis **10.** _____ sacar la basura todas las noches. Y

Azucena **11.** _____ ayudar a preparar la cena. Todos nuestros hijos

12. _____ organizar sus cuartos. Yo **13.** _____ lavar los

platos después de cenar. Y tú y yo **14.** _____ caminar con el perro después

de cenar.

SCORE [ ]

Alternative Quiz 6-3A

C. There is a lot of work to be done at Arturo's house. Complete the statements about what everyone should do with the correct form of **deber** and the missing infinitives from the box. (16 points)

planchar	pasar	cortar	hacer
limpiar	trabajar	cuidar	poner

15. ¡Qué feo está el patio! Nosotros _____ _____ en el jardín por la tarde, ¿verdad?

16. No hay ropa limpia en mi armario. _____ _____ la ropa ahora.

17. Lola no debe estar sola *(alone)*. Josué _____ _____ a ella.

18. ¿Y quiénes _____ _____ la mesa?

19. ¡La sala es un desastre! Antonieta _____ _____ la aspiradora ahora mismo.

20. Y después, yo _____ _____ la cocina.

21. Lucero, tú y yo _____ _____ las camas, ¿no?

22. Juan Antonio _____ _____ el césped.

SCORE [ ]

TOTAL SCORE [ ] /30

Nombre _____ Clase _____ Fecha _____

¿Qué te gustaría hacer?

PRIMER PASO

Maximum Score: 30

Grammar and Vocabulary

A. Different members of Bartolomé's family are returning home from excursions. Write out his explanations of where each person or group is coming from, using the correct forms of **venir** and the Spanish words for the places pictured. (10 points)

1. Bartolomé

_____

_____

2. Mamá y Papá

_____

_____

3. Toño

_____

_____

4. Roberta y yo

_____

_____

5. Mis primos

_____

_____

SCORE _____

CAPITULO 7

Alternative Quiz 7-1A

B. Rosaura and Enrique are making plans for this afternoon. Complete their conversation with the correct forms of the verbs **empezar, preferir**, and **venir**. (12 points)

ROSAURA   Enrique, voy al cine esta tarde. ¿Quieres ir conmigo?

ENRIQUE   ¿A qué hora **6.** _____ la película?

ROSAURA   A las cinco.

ENRIQUE   Pues... gracias, pero yo **7.** _____ ir contigo otro día, si es posible. Hoy después de clase Arturo y Renata **8.** _____ a mi casa a estudiar para el examen de historia.

ROSAURA   Pero el examen de historia es el jueves, y hoy es lunes. ¿Por qué

9. _____ ustedes a estudiar hoy? Todavía es muy temprano, ¿no?

ENRIQUE   Pues, los exámenes de historia siempre son difíciles, y nosotros

10. _____ estar preparados. Oye, ¿por qué no

11. _____ tú a mi casa también?

ROSAURA   Bueno, de acuerdo. ¿Está bien si yo **12.** _____ a las cuatro?

ENRIQUE   Perfecto, entonces nosotros **13.** _____ a estudiar a las cuatro y quince.

SCORE [   ]

C. Complete the descriptions of people's activities with the correct forms of the verb in parentheses. (8 points)

—José Luis, el sábado tú **14.** _____ (empezar) con tu nueva clase de arte, ¿verdad? ¿Qué **15.** _____ (preferir) hacer en tu tiempo libre, dibujar o pintar?

—La fiesta de Úrsula **16.** _____ (empezar) a las ocho. Sus primas Daniela y Alicia **17.** _____ (venir) a la fiesta, pero ellas **18.** _____ (preferir) llegar un poco tarde, a las nueve.

—Típicamente yo **19.** _____ (empezar) la tarea a las cuatro y media. A veces mi amiga Ana María **20.** _____ (venir) a casa a estudiar conmigo. Nosotros **21.** _____ (preferir) escuchar la radio cuando estudiamos.

SCORE [   ]

TOTAL SCORE [   ] /30

Spanish 1 ¡Ven conmigo!, Chapter 7

7 ¿Qué te gustaría hacer?

Alternative Quiz 7-2A

Maximum Score: 35

■ SEGUNDO PASO

Grammar and Vocabulary

A. Darío is talking about everyone's daily routine. Complete each sentence with the correct form of the underlined verb. Remember to use the correct reflexive pronoun. (9 points)

1. Los fines de semana, mi hermano prefiere no <u>afeitarse</u>. Pero mi papá necesita

   _____ todos los días.

2. Mi hermana prefiere <u>maquillarse</u> todos los días. Pero mi mamá prefiere

   _____ sólo para las fiestas. Y tú, Aurora, a ti no te gusta

   _____, ¿verdad?

3. Mi hermano prefiere <u>lavarse</u> los dientes antes de desayunar. Yo prefiero

   _____ los dientes después.

4. Prefiero <u>ducharme</u> por la mañana. Elena, ¿cuándo quieres _____? ¿Y cuándo

   necesita _____ Juanita?

   SCORE [_____]

B. Adolfo is talking to his family while everyone gets ready to go out. Complete what he says with the correct missing verb. Use each verb only once. (10 points)

> peinarte   lavarte los dientes   afeitarme
> ducharse   maquillarse

Sylvia, date prisa porque yo todavía necesito _____. Azucena, ¿qué
                                                              5.

comes? Necesitas _____ ahora mismo. ¡Y mira tu pelo! Vas a
                         6.

_____ ahora, ¿verdad? Mamá todavía quiere
        7.

_____, y creo que Papá necesita _____ después.
        8.   9.

   SCORE [_____]

Alternative Quiz 7-2A

C. Leonor y Francisca are talking about weekend plans. Complete their conversation about what is going to happen, using the correct form of the expression **ir + a** and a logical infinitive. Some infinitives may be used more than once. (7 points)

asistir	tener	hacer	visitar
	ver	ir	

LEONOR   ¿Qué haces este fin de semana? ¿**10.** _____ a tus abuelos?

FRANCISCA   Sí. Mis primos y yo **11.** _____ una fiesta grande para mi

abuela. Ella **12.** _____ 80 años. ¿Y qué planes tienes tú?

LEONOR   **13.** _____ al parque de atracciones con Ernestina el sábado.

Después, creo que nosotras **14.** _____ una película.

FRANCISCA   ¿Y alguien más **15.** _____ con ustedes?

LEONOR   No. Amparo necesita ir a una boda. Y creo que Rogelio y Georgina

16. _____ a un concierto.

SCORE [   ]

D. Your friend Verónica sent you a note about what everyone is doing for the surprise party for a classmate. Complete the note with the correct form of **pensar.** (9 points)

¡Hola! Tú, ¿qué **17.** _____ hacer para la fiesta? Romero y Esmeralda

18. _____ limpiar la sala. Y Rosario **19.** _____ tocar la gui-

tarra. Gabriela y yo **20.** _____ comprar la comida. Yo también

21. _____ invitar a unos amigos. La fiesta es a las ocho en punto, pero todos

nosotros **22.** _____ estar allí a las ocho menos cuarto.

SCORE [   ]

TOTAL SCORE [   ] /35

7 ¿Qué te gustaría hacer?

Alternative Quiz 7-3A

■ TERCER PASO

Maximum Score: 35

Grammar and Vocabulary

A. Read each sentence. Then, use an expression with **tener** to complete the summarizing statements in Spanish. Remember to use the correct form of **tener.** (18 points)

1. Your friend has a big math test tomorrow.

   Él _____ estudiar mucho esta noche.

2. Alberto and Mateo have to practice for the meet on Saturday.

   Ellos _____ practicar.

3. Claudia and Julieta have class at 2:15. It's now 2:14.

   Ellas _____.

4. You and your friends would love to go for pizza after class.

   Nosotros _____ comer pizza.

5. Irma and Rodolfo want to go to the mall after school.

   Ellos _____ comprar ropa nueva.

6. Luis Enrique has a cavity every time he goes to the dentist.

   Él _____ lavarse los dientes más.

7. You woke up late, and need to shower and get dressed in ten minutes.

   Yo _____ mucha _____.

8. Last night you stayed up until 3:00 A.M.

   Hoy _____ mucho _____.

9. Your friend Berta has her 16th birthday today.

   Hoy ella _____ 16 _____.

SCORE [   ]

CAPÍTULO 7

Alternative Quiz 7-3A

B. This weekend, everyone has responsibilities that conflict with their fun plans. First explain what everyone feels like doing, then write what that person has to do. Use the correct expressions with **tener** and the infinitives in parentheses. (10 points)

10. el profesor (ir al campo, trabajar)

_____, pero _____.

11. yo (ver una película, cuidar a mi hermanita)

_____, pero _____.

12. mis amigos y yo (comer hamburguesas, estudiar)

_____, pero _____.

13. tú (tomar un refresco, organizar tu cuarto)

_____, pero _____.

14. Juan Domingo y Eufemia (asistir al baile, visitar a sus tíos)

_____, pero _____.

SCORE [   ]

C. Juan David and Óscar are trying to make plans for the weekend. Complete their conversation with the missing expressions. Each expression will be used only once. (7 points)

Qué lástima	ocupado	cita	lo siento	
tengo planes		Tal vez	Te gustaría	

JUAN DAVID   Óscar, ¿qué haces el sábado? ¿15. _____ ir conmigo al

partido?

ÓSCAR   Gracias, pero ya 16. _____ para el sábado.

¿17. _____ el domingo?

JUAN DAVID   Ay, 18. _____, pero el domingo es imposible. Estoy

19. _____ todo el día. Y por la noche tengo una

20. _____ con Teresa.

ÓSCAR   ¡21. _____! Pues, otro día entonces.

SCORE [   ]

TOTAL SCORE [   ] /35

Spanish 1 ¡Ven conmigo!, Chapter 7

CAPÍTULO 8

¡A comer!

PRIMER PASO

Maximum Score: 35

Grammar and Vocabulary

A. Complete the statements about what everyone does for lunch with the correct form of the verb **almorzar.** (5 points)

1. Este fin de semana, mi primo Mauricio _____ con nosotros.

2. ¿Tú siempre _____ en la cafetería también?

3. Los domingos, mis padres y yo _____ con mis abuelos.

4. Durante la semana, yo _____ con mis amigos Ramiro y Lucía casi siempre.

5. Típicamente, mis abuelos _____ a las dos o tres de la tarde.

SCORE _____

B. Everyone in Mario's family is allergic to something. Complete his statements about what different people can't eat with the correct form of the verb **poder.** (4 points)

6. Mamá y yo no _____ comer crema de maní.

7. Mis primos no _____ tomar leche.

8. Mi hermano mayor no _____ comer chocolate.

9. Yo no _____ comer papayas.

SCORE _____

C. Some friends are wondering where to go for lunch, since everyone likes different kinds of food. Complete their conversation with the correct indirect object pronouns and the correct form of **encantar** or **gustar.** (16 points)

RAÚL   Pues, a mí 10. _____ 11. _____ la pizza y las

hamburguesas.

LEO   A mí 12. _____ 13. _____ la pizza con queso,

pero no 14. _____ 15. _____ para nada las ham-

burguesas. Antonio, ¿qué prefieres almorzar? ¿A ti 16. _____

17. _____ la pizza?

Alternative Quiz 8-1A

ANTONIO Sí, 18. _____ 19. _____ la comida italiana. Es mi

comida favorita.

LEO ¿Y qué 20. _____ 21. _____ comer a Genoveva?

RAÚL Creo que 22. _____ 23. _____ la comida china.

Ella es vegetariana, entonces no 24. _____

25. _____ las hamburguesas.

SCORE [   ]

D. It's lunchtime, and Rosa María and Juan Alberto are talking about food. Complete their conversation with the missing words. Each word will be used once. (10 points)

toronja	papitas	plátano	sopa		cereal
	pan tostado	ligeros	almuerzo	fuertes	queso

ROSA MARÍA ¿Qué tienes para el 26. _____ hoy?

JUAN ALBERTO A ver... Pues, un sándwich de jamón y 27. _____, unas

28. _____ y una manzana. ¿Y tú?

ROSA MARÍA Hoy voy a comprar el almuerzo. Tengo ganas de comer

29. _____ de pollo y una ensalada de frutas con

30. _____, papaya y 31. _____.

JUAN ALBERTO A mí me gusta la fruta para el desayuno. ¿Y tú? ¿Prefieres los desayunos

32. _____?

ROSA MARÍA No, me gustan más los desayunos 33. _____. Por ejemplo,

me encanta el 34. _____ con leche. A veces como

35. _____ con jalea también.

SCORE [   ]

TOTAL SCORE [/35]

CAPÍTULO 8

¡A comer!

SEGUNDO PASO

Grammar and Vocabulary

A. While eating at a restaurant, Raquel and Enriqueta are talking about different foods. Complete their conversation with the correct form of **ser** or **estar**. (16 points)

RAQUEL   En el verano, siempre como ensaladas de frutas. **1.** _____ deli-

ciosas. Me encantan las comidas frías cuando hace calor.

ENRIQUETA   Yo prefiero las comidas calientes. Creo que las sopas

2. _____ muy ricas, especialmente la sopa de pollo.

RAQUEL   ¿Y cómo **3.** _____ tu sopa hoy?

ENRIQUETA   Pues, **4.** _____ un poco salada. ¿Cómo

5. _____ los frijoles?

RAQUEL   **6.** _____ picantes, pero así me gustan. En general la comida

picante **7.** _____ mi favorita. Los frijoles que prepara mi

abuela **8.** _____ los más ricos del mundo.

SCORE [   ]

B. Complete the statements made by diners at a restaurant with the correct Spanish adjectives. Remember to make the adjectives agree with the nouns they refer to. (8 points)

—¡Ay! ¡Qué **9.** _____ y **10.** _____ están las enchiladas!
       (spicy)   *(salty)*

Necesito un vaso de agua **11.** _____, por favor.
                              (cold)

—Los postres aquí son todos **12.** _____. Me encanta el flan de vainilla.
                                 (delicious)

Es muy **13.** _____.
            (sweet)

—Este té está **14.** _____. Quiero un té **15.** _____, por favor.
                   (hot)   *(cold)*

—¡Mmm! Hoy la sopa de legumbres está **16.** _____.
                                          (delicious)

SCORE [   ]

Alternative Quiz 8-2A

C. Read each situation, then write a statement or question summarizing it using the Spanish expressions for *to be hungry* or *to be thirsty*. Remember to use the correct form of the verb. (6 points)

17. Your little sister never drinks her juice at breakfast.

    Ella no _____.

18. Adriana and María Luisa just finished going for a run on a hot summer afternoon.

    Ellas _____.

19. You skipped breakfast, and it's now almost noon.

    Yo _____.

20. You and your friends decide to go for ice cream at the mall.

    Nosotros _____.

21. Your friend Ernesto just bought three hamburgers for lunch.

    Él _____.

22. You wonder why your friend Delia Alicia isn't eating her lunch today.

    Delia Alicia, ¿no_____?

SCORE [   ]

TOTAL SCORE [/30]

CAPÍTULO 8

¡A comer!

■ TERCER PASO

Maximum Score: 35

Grammar and Vocabulary

A. You're at a restaurant with your nephew Pepito, who is four years old and pretty mischievous. Complete what you say to Pepito and the waiter with the correct form of **otro**. (7 points)

¡Ay, Pepito! Camarero, ¿nos puede traer **1.** _____ tenedores, por favor?

¡Ay, no! Y también **2.** _____ cuchara y **3.** _____ vaso de

leche. Y ahora, ¿qué? Camarero, ¿nos trae también **4.** _____ ensalada y

5. _____ servilletas? Pepito, mira a los **6.** _____ niños aquí.

Ellos son buenos y no hacen esas cosas malas. Y aquí viene el camarero con

7. _____ postre para ti. Por favor, pórtate bien *(behave)*.

SCORE _____

B. Complete the statements and requests made by diners at a restaurant with the missing words and expressions. Each expression will be used only once. (9 points)

| voy a pedir | Qué le puedo traer | Está incluida | Quisiera |
| limpia | sucia | vas a pedir | Desea algo más | cuenta |

—Camarero, necesito una servilleta **8.** _____, por favor. Esta

servilleta está **9.** _____.

—Elsa, ¿tienes allí la **10.** _____? ¿Cuánto es?
—Son 34 dólares.

—¿Es todo? ¿**11.** _____ la propina?

—Carlos, aquí viene el camarero. ¿Qué **12.** _____?

—Creo que **13.** _____ el pescado.

—Buenas tardes, señor. ¿**14.** _____?

—**15.** _____ el bistec con papas fritas.

—Muy bien. ¿**16.** _____?
—Sí, una ensalada de lechuga y tomate.

SCORE _____

Alternative Quiz 8-3A

C. For a health class project, you polled students on what they ate. Now explain how many of the following items are consumed by your classmates in a year, using the data from the poll below. Write all numbers as words. (12 points)

plátanos	591	bistecs	842
uvas	168.311	sándwiches	11.913
ensaladas	655	refrescos	2.147
papitas	36.740	batidos	4.831

En un año, los estudiantes de mi colegio comen...

17. _____ plátanos.

18. _____ uvas.

19. _____ ensaladas.

20. _____ papitas.

21. _____ bistecs.

22. _____ sándwiches.

Ellos toman...

23. _____ refrescos.

24. _____ batidos.

SCORE [   ]

D. Write the Spanish word for the item you would need to do the following things. Include the indefinite article. (7 points)

25. eat soup or ice cream _____

26. eat peas or twirl spaghetti _____

27. wipe your hands _____

28. serve lemonade _____

29. put your cereal and milk in _____

30. slice carrots and tomatoes for a salad _____

31. eat your sandwich off of _____

SCORE [   ]

TOTAL SCORE [   ] /30

Spanish 1 ¡Ven conmigo!, Chapter 8

Nombre _____ Clase _____ Fecha _____

CAPÍTULO 9

¡Vamos de compras!

Alternative Quiz 9-1 A

Maximum Score: 30

■ PRIMER PASO

Grammar and Vocabulary

A. Read the statements about what people need to buy and which stores they need to visit, then complete each one with the correct missing word. (15 points)

juguetes	flores	zapatería	dulcería	tarjeta	joyería
corbata	tienda de comestibles			aretes	pastelería

1. Papá necesita una _____ nueva. ¿Quieres ir conmigo al almacén más tarde?

2. Pienso ir a la _____ para comprar el regalo de abuela. A ella le encanta el chocolate.

3. Quiero comprarle una _____ cómica a Maricela. ¿Tienes ganas de ir conmigo a la papelería?

4. Busco un collar para mi hermana. Voy a la _____ hoy.

5. Hijos, vamos a la _____ esta tarde. Necesitamos pan, leche y fruta.

6. Mamá, necesito unos zapatos para ir al baile. ¿Puedo ir a la _____ esta tarde?

7. Tengo ganas de comer algo dulce, como unas galletas o un pastel de manzana. Pienso ir a la _____ después de clases.

8. Quiero comprarle unas _____ a mamá. Voy a la florería mañana.

9. Buscas unos _____ para Tina, ¿verdad? Si quieres, voy contigo a la juguetería este fin de semana.

10. Para el regalo de mi prima, necesito ir a la joyería. Voy a comprarle unos _____.

SCORE [   ]

B. Complete the statements about what you are going to give people on their birthdays with the correct indirect object pronoun. (6 points)

11. Marta y Mario, a ustedes _____ voy a regalar unos carteles.

12. Mamá, a ti _____ voy a regalar unos aretes.

13. A mis hermanas _____ voy a regalar unos dulces.

14. A ti _____ voy a regalar un disco compacto.

15. A mi primo _____ voy a regalar una novela.

16. A mi padre _____ voy a regalar una planta.

SCORE [   ]

CAPÍTULO 9

Alternative Quiz 9-1A

Now explain what people are going to give you and your friends for your next birthdays by completing the statements with the correct indirect object pronoun. (6 points)

17. Mi abuelo _____ va a regalar un libro.

18. Y a mi hermano y a mí _____ va a regalar un juego de mesa.

19. A Rosalba y a mí _____ van a regalar un radio.

20. Mi hermano _____ va a regalar unas revistas.

21. Mis padres _____ van a regalar unas zapatillas de tenis.

22. A Salvador y a mí _____ van a regalar unas camisetas.

SCORE _____

C. Look at the map of downtown, then complete the directions by underlining the correct expressions. (8 points)

23. La pastelería queda (cerca del/a tres cuadras del) parque.

24. Correos y la juguetería quedan al lado del (parque/almacén).

25. La tienda de comestibles está (cerca de/lejos de) la universidad.

26. La dulcería está (lejos de/encima de) la tienda de comestibles.

27. La zapatería queda (debajo de/a dos cuadras de) la dulcería.

28. La florería queda (al lado del/encima del) museo.

29. La juguetería está (a dos cuadras del/lejos del) almacén.

30. La panadería queda a tres cuadras del (café/museo).

SCORE _____

TOTAL SCORE _____ /30

Spanish 1 ¡Ven conmigo!, Chapter 9

CAPÍTULO 9

¡Vamos de compras!

■ SEGUNDO PASO

Grammar and Vocabulary

A. Read what Delia says about two local stores, Almacenes Peña and Boutique Rosa. Then make comparisons between the two stores, based on what you've read and using the correct form of the adjectives in parentheses. (10 points)

Almacenes Peña	Boutique Rosa
Es enorme. Tienen mucha ropa.	No tienen mucha ropa allí.
Los precios son altos.	Los precios son bajos.
Me gustan las personas que trabajan allí.	¡Uf! ¡Qué antipáticos son todos!
La ropa formal allí es muy elegante.	También es muy elegante su ropa formal.
Está muy lejos de mi casa.	Está al lado de mi casa.

1. el almacén/la boutique (grande)

_____

2. la ropa en la Boutique Rosa/la ropa en los Almacenes Peña (caro)

_____

3. Las personas que trabajan en el almacén/las personas que trabajan en la boutique (simpático)

_____

4. la ropa formal en el almacén/la ropa formal en la boutique (elegante)

_____

5. el almacén/la boutique (cerca)

_____

SCORE _____

B. Tell your friend Marisol about the unusual clothing you found at a thrift store. Write the Spanish expressions for the items below. (6 points)

6. a pink suit _____

7. a green belt _____

8. a plaid jacket _____

9. some striped socks _____

SCORE _____

CAPÍTULO 9

Alternative Quiz 9-2A

C. You work in a department store. Tell customers what the items below are made of. Choose a logical material for each item and use the correct expression with **ser.** (9 points)

cuero	algodón
lana	seda

10. cartera _____

11. botas _____

12. corbata _____

13. calcetines de tenis _____

14. suéteres de esquí _____

15. camisetas para niños _____

SCORE [ ]

D. What does everyone want to buy at the clothing store? Write the correct Spanish word for the items pictured. Include the indefinite articles. (10 points)

16.  _____ 21.  _____

17.  _____ 22.  _____

18.  _____ 23. _____

19.  _____ 24. _____

20. 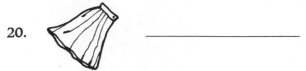 _____ 25. _____

SCORE [ ]

TOTAL SCORE [/35]

Spanish 1 ¡Ven conmigo!, Chapter 9

CAPÍTULO 9

CAPÍTULO

9

¡Vamos de compras!

■ TERCER PASO

Grammar and Vocabulary

A. What Spanish expression would you use to say that something is . . .? (6 points)

1. cheap _____

2. a bargain _____

3. expensive _____

4. a rip-off _____

SCORE [   ]

B. Complete these statements made by shoppers at a department store with the correct Spanish forms of the demonstrative adjectives. (15 points)

—5. _____ vestido es muy bonito, ¿no? Y me gustan mucho
      (That)

6. _____ blusas blancas.
   (these)

—¿Qué compro para ir a la playa? Me gustan 7. _____ traje de baño y
                                               (this)

8. _____ camisetas. Y me encantan 9. _____ sandalias allí.
   (these)   *(those)*

—Mira... me gusta 10. _____ falda. Pero 11. _____
                      (this)   *(those)*

pantalones son horribles.

—Voy a comprar 12. _____ cinturón, pero no quiero 13. _____,
                   (this)   *(those)*

corbatas. Pienso comprar 14. _____ camisa también.
                             (that)

SCORE [   ]

C
A
P
Í
T
U
L
O

9

Alternative Quiz 9-3A

C. Flor and her friends are window-shopping. Use **cuesta** or **cuestan** to complete what they say about the prices of the things they see. (6 points)

15. ¡Mira! ¡Ese vestido _____ 400 dólares!

16. Esos zapatos son muy elegantes, ¿no? ¿Cuánto _____?

17. ¿Ves esos bluejeans allí? ¿Cuánto _____?

18. Esa blusa de seda _____ 60 dólares. Es cara, pero me gusta mucho.

19. Me gusta mucho esa chaqueta. ¿Cuánto _____?

20. Necesito unas camisetas, pero aquí _____ 30 dólares. Es mucho, ¿no?

SCORE _____

D. Leonor and Clara are shopping at a vintage clothing store. Complete their conversation with the clerk with the missing expressions. Use each expression only once. (8 points)

prefiero	Cuál de	la gris	cuesta	Además
Te queda	Cuánto cuestan			me gusta más

LEONOR Perdón, señorita. ¿ _____ estas faldas?
  21.

CLERK La negra cuesta 15 dólares. La falda gris _____ 12 dólares.
  22.

LEONOR Gracias. Laura, mira... ¿ _____ estas faldas prefieres? ¿La negra o
  23.

  _____?
  24.

CLARA Este... pues, creo que _____ la negra.
  25.

LEONOR A mí también _____.
  26.

CLERK _____ muy bien. _____, el negro es un color
  27. 28.

  muy elegante.

SCORE _____

TOTAL SCORE _____ /35

Spanish 1 ¡Ven conmigo!, Chapter 9

CAPÍTULO 9

Celebraciones

■ PRIMER PASO

Maximum Score: 35

Grammar and Vocabulary

A. Rubí and her brother Juan are getting ready for their mom's birthday party. Complete their conversation with the missing expressions. (9 points)

Crees que	está decorando	qué te parece si
creo que no	Me parece bien	Estoy colgando

RUBÍ   Juan, ¿qué haces ahora? Necesito tu ayuda.

JUAN   Un momento. 1. _____ las decoraciones.

RUBÍ   ¿Por qué no 2. _____ la sala Elena?

JUAN   Porque necesita ayudar a papá en la cocina. Oye, ¿3. _____ ponemos unas sillas afuera, en el patio?

RUBÍ   4. _____. ¿Y qué hacemos con el pastel y los refrescos?

         ¿5._____ debemos ponerlos en el patio también?

JUAN   No, 6. _____. Prefiero poner la comida en la sala.

SCORE _____

B. Read the statements, then complete the sentences about what each person or group is doing right now. Use the correct form of the present progressive and choose from the infinitives below. (14 points)

hacer la tarea	buscar un regalo	organizar su cuarto
poner la mesa	leer el libro de español	beber agua comer sándwiches

7. Concha y yo tenemos hambre.

   Ella y yo _____.

8. El cuarto de Marcelo está sucio.

   Él _____.

9. Tengo un examen de español mañana.

   Yo _____.

Alternative Quiz 10-1A

10. Vamos a cenar en cinco minutos.

   Tú y papá _____.

11. Siempre hay mucha tarea en nuestra clase de ciencias.

   Mi amigo y yo _____.

12. La mamá de Gustavo tiene un cumpleaños mañana.

   Gustavo _____.

13. Pedro y Mariana tienen mucha sed después de la clase de aeróbicos.

   Ellos _____.

SCORE _____

C. Read the sentences and decide which U.S. holiday each one describes. Write the Spanish name for the holiday. You may use some holidays more than once. (12 points)

14. Es en el mes de febrero. _____

15. Casi siempre comen pavo *(turkey)* ese día. _____

16. Es en el mes de junio. _____

17. Es en el otoño. _____

18. Muchas ciudades celebran este día festivo con fuegos artificiales *(fireworks)*.

   _____

19. Es en el invierno. _____

20. Es en el mes de mayo. _____

21. Es en el mes de julio. _____

22. Celebramos estos dos días festivos en dos años diferentes. _____,

   _____

23. Muchas personas celebran este día con regalos y un árbol *(tree)* decorado.

   _____

24. Lo celebran en la primavera con huevos pintados, dulces y ropa nueva.

   _____

SCORE _____

TOTAL SCORE _____ /35

10 Celebraciones

Alternative Quiz 10-2A

■ SEGUNDO PASO

Maximum Score: 35

Grammar and Vocabulary

A. Celestina is babysitting her younger brother and sister for a weekend while her parents are out of town. Complete the instructions her parents left for Celestina, Linda, and David with the correct informal command. Use the verbs in parentheses. (20 points)

Celestina:

1. _____ (Preparar) espaguetis y una ensalada para la cena el sábado.

2. _____ (Ayudar) a Linda con su tarea.

3. _____ (Lavar) la ropa de Linda y David.

Linda:

4. _____ (Hacer) tu tarea de matemáticas.

5. _____ (Poner) la mesa el viernes y el sábado.

6. _____ (Ir) a visitar a tu abuela el domingo.

7. _____ (Limpiar) tu cuarto.

David:

8. _____ (Cuidar) al gato el viernes y el sábado.

9. _____ (Sacar) la basura todos los días.

10. _____ (Cortar) el césped el sábado.

SCORE _____

CAPÍTULO 10

Alternative Quiz 10-2A

B. Complete the requests and responses people make before a surprise party with the correct missing expression. (7 points)

un momentito	me haces el favor de	me ayudas a
cómo no	Lo siento traes	Perdóname

—Sergio, pasa la aspiradora, ¿quieres?

—**11.** _____, pero en este momento estoy limpiando la cocina.

—Rafael, ¿**12.** _____ llamar a la pastelería?

—Sí, **13.** _____, pero primero necesito colgar las decoraciones.

—Lenora, ¿**14.** _____ preparar los sándwiches esta tarde?

—**15.** _____, pero no puedo. Esta tarde tengo clase de baile.

—Amalia, me **16.** _____ esas sillas, ¿por favor?

—Sí, **17.** _____. ¿Las pongo en la sala?   SCORE [____]

C. You need some help getting ready for a party. Read the situations, then use the expressions below to ask a friend for help with each problem. (8 points)

mandar las invitaciones	inflar los globos	poner los regalos en el cuarto
pasar las decoraciones	poner las sillas en la sala	colgar los globos
ayudar a limpiar la casa		traer helado y galletas

18. You can't reach the box of decorations. _____

19. You have a lot of invitations to address and send. _____

20. You need more food for dessert. _____

21. You need help cleaning the house. _____

22. You want to hang balloons outside and all over the house. _____

23. There aren't enough chairs in the living room. _____

24. After the party, all the gifts need to be put in the bedroom. _____

25. You need to blow up 50 balloons. _____

SCORE [____]

TOTAL SCORE [____] /35

10 Celebraciones

CAPÍTULO 10

■ TERCER PASO

Maximum Score: 30

Grammar and Vocabulary

A. Juan David wrote a description of what his family did to celebrate Thanksgiving this past year. Complete his description with the correct preterite forms of the verbs in parentheses. (15 points)

Nosotros _____ el Día de Acción de Gracias el 27 de noviembre. Todos
      1. (celebrar)

_____ con las preparaciones. Mamá y la tía Tere _____
   2. (ayudar)   **3. (preparar)**

mucha comida. Y mi papá _____ nuestro postre favorito, pastel de calabaza
              4. (hacer)

(pumpkin). Mis hermanos Rosaura y Esteban _____ la casa. Carlitos, mi her-
              5. (decorar)

mano menor, los _____ . Yo _____ a mis amigos Pancho y
      6. (ayudar)   **7. (invitar)**

Ana a cenar con nosotros. Ellos _____ a las cuatro de la tarde. Nosotros
              8. (llegar)

_____ a las seis. Después, yo _____ a mis primos en San
   9. (cenar)   **10. (llamar)**

Antonio para desearles *(to wish them)* un feliz Día de Acción de Gracias.

SCORE [ ]

B. Lucinda's mom is asking her daughter if she's done all the things she was supposed to do this afternoon. Write Lucinda's answers to her mom's questions, using the correct preterite form of the verbs and the correct direct object pronoun. (10 points)

11. ¿Cortaste el césped? (sí)

_____

12. ¿Y ayudaste a tu papá con el carro? (sí)

_____

13. Lucinda, ¿ya lavaste la ropa? (sí)

_____

Alternative Quiz 10-3A

14. ¿Y compraste el pan para la cena? (no)

_____

15. ¿Limpiaste tu cuarto? (no)

_____

SCORE [ ]

C. Today is the 18th, the day of Aurora's party. Complete the statements by explaining when she did things to get ready. Use the Spanish expressions for *last night, yesterday, the day before yesterday, last week,* and *last Saturday.* Look at Aurora's calendar to decide which expression to use. (5 points)

lunes	martes	miércoles	jueves	viernes	sábado	domingo
6 hacer listas de invitados y comida	**7** hacer listas de invitados y comida	**8** hacer listas de invitados y comida	**9** hacer listas de invitados y comida	**10** hacer listas de invitados y comida	**11** llamar a los invitados	**12**
13	**14**	**15**	**16** limpiar la casa	**17** comprar la comida ____ preparar la comida	**18** ¡FIESTA!	**19**

1. Aurora preparó la comida _____.

2. _____ compró la comida.

3. Llamó a los invitados _____.

4. _____ ella limpió la casa.

5. _____ Aurora hizo las listas de los invitados y

la comida.

SCORE [ ]

TOTAL SCORE [/30]

11 Para vivir bien

Alternative Quiz 11-1A

Maximum Score: 30

■ PRIMER PASO

Grammar and Vocabulary

A. Read each situation, then complete the statements about how each person or group feels with the correct form of **sentirse**. Remember to use the correct reflexive pronoun. (12 points)

1. ¡Uf! Estudié hasta las doce de la noche anoche.

   Hoy _____ mal.

2. Tú no descansaste mucho este fin de semana, ¿verdad?

   ¿Todavía _____ cansado?

3. Ayer Salvador y Héctor jugaron al basquetbol por cuatro horas.

   Ellos _____ cansados.

4. Mi hermano y yo comemos bien y hacemos ejercicio todos los días.

   Nosotros _____ muy bien.

5. Arturo y Lourdes, ¿por qué tomaron ustedes tantos refrescos y helados ayer?

   Hoy ustedes _____ muy mal, ¿verdad?

6. Mariana lleva una vida muy sana.

   Ella casi siempre _____ bien.

SCORE _____

B. Complete each statement about what people are doing and saying in the health club today with the correct reflexive pronoun. (10 points)

—Diego y Juana siempre **7.** _____ estiran antes y después de su clase de ejercicio.

—¡La clase de yoga es fabulosa! Nosotros **8.** _____ sentimos muy bien después de esa clase.

—Mauricio, ¿por qué **9.** _____ peinas antes de hacer ejercicio? ¿Por qué no

   10. _____ lavas el pelo después?

—Hola, Hortensia y Marisol. ¿Cómo **11.** _____ sienten ustedes? ¿Listas

   (ready) para la clase?

—No voy a ir a la clase de natación hoy. No **12.** _____ siento bien.

Alternative Quiz 11-1A

—Después de levantar pesas, Lucila **13.** _____ ducha y

14. _____ maquilla en el baño del gimnasio.

—Carlitos, **15.** _____ vas a duchar antes de nadar, ¿verdad?

—Diana, ¿por qué vas a correr ahora? No **16.** _____ sientes cansada?

SCORE [   ]

C. Write a sentence explaining what each person or group in the picture does for exercise. Use a different verb in each sentence. (8 points)

MODELO   Gonzalo y Juan Ricardo corren después de clases.

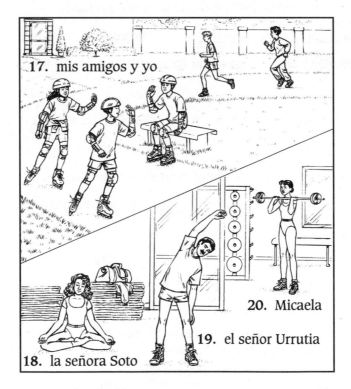

17. mis amigos y yo

20. Micaela

19. el señor Urrutia

18. la señora Soto

17. _____

18. _____

19. _____

20. _____

SCORE [   ]

TOTAL SCORE [   ] /30

Spanish 1 ¡Ven conmigo!, Chapter 11

CAPÍTULO 11

Para vivir bien

■ SEGUNDO PASO

Maximum Score: 35

Grammar and Vocabulary

A. While at the gym, people are talking about different aches and pains. Complete their conversations with the correct pronouns and forms of **doler.** (14 points)

—Héctor y yo no vamos a correr hoy. A nosotros dos _____

_____ las piernas.
　　　　2.

—A Sonia y a Vicente _____ _____ las piernas también,
　　　　　　　　　　　3.　　　　　　　　　4.

porque montaron en bicicleta por tres horas ayer.

—¡La instructora de aeróbicos es increíble! Nunca se cansa, y parece que nunca

_____ _____ nada.
　　　5.　　　　　　　6.

—Antonieta, ¿a ti _____ _____ la espalda después de
　　　　　　　　　　7.　　　　　　　　8.

levantar pesas?

—No, pero a veces _____ _____ los brazos.
　　　　　　　　　9.　　　　　　　10.

—Doña Flor, usted toma una clase de yoga, ¿verdad? ¿Todavía _____
　　　　　　　　　　　　　　　　　　　　　　　　　　　　　11.

_____ el cuello?
　　12.

—No, ya no _____ _____ nada. Estoy muy bien,
　　　　　　　13.　　　　　　　14.

gracias.

SCORE _____

Alternative Quiz 11-2A

B. Read each statement, then summarize how each person feels using a logical expression with **tener** or **estar.** Use a different expression for each situation. (9 points)

15. Lourdes está en el baño, buscando el termómetro *(thermometer)* y unas aspirinas.

_____

16. A Alfonso le duele la garganta. _____

17. Esta tarde voy al médico para una inyección *(shot).* ¡No me gustan nada las inyecciones!

_____

18. Ramiro no puede respirar *(to breathe)* bien, y se siente cansado.

_____

19. Adolfo y yo nos sentimos muy mal. Tenemos frío y calor al mismo tiempo *(at the same time),* y nos duele todo el cuerpo. _____

20. Víctor y Mario no pueden jugar en el partido de voleibol hoy. Están enfermos y tienen que estar en casa. _____

SCORE [   ]

C. Little Gilberto is just learning the words for body parts. Help him by completing the explananation with the correct missing word. (12 points)

piernas	cabeza	manos	oídos
ojos	brazos	dedos	boca

Gilberto, el pelo está encima de la _____. Los _____ son
                                            21.   22.

para escuchar, y la _____ es para hablar y comer. Tienes dos
                          23.

_____ para ver las cosas. Y mira… necesitas las _____ para
          24.   25.

dibujar y pintar. En cada una, hay cinco _____. Usas los _____
                                              26.   27.

para levantar cosas y las _____ para correr y montar en bici.
                                28.

SCORE [   ]

TOTAL SCORE [   ] /35

CAPÍTULO 11 **Para vivir bien**

■ **TERCER PASO**

Maximum Score: 35

Grammar and Vocabulary

A. Everyone in Hortensia's family did something athletic this week. Complete the sentences about where everyone went with the correct preterite form of **ir** in the first blank, and the most logical place for that sport or activity in the second blank. Mention each place only once. 14 points)

1. El sábado, mis hermanos _____ a las _____ para jugar al fútbol con unos amigos.

2. Mi tío _____ al _____ para ver un partido de béisbol el domingo.

3. Ernesto y yo _____ a las _____ para jugar al tenis el viernes.

4. Ayer por la tarde, yo _____ a la _____ para hacer atletismo *(track and field)*.

5. Y mi abuela y sus dos perros _____ al _____ para caminar y ver a las personas.

6. ¿Cuándo _____ tú a la _____ para nadar? ¿Ayer o anteayer?

7. Leonor _____ al _____ para levantar pesas anoche.

SCORE [   ]

B. Sandro is talking about the fun he had last week. Complete what he says with the missing preterite forms of **jugar.** (9 points)

El lunes pasado Ernesto y yo _____ al tenis en el parque. Más tarde, yo
                                            8.

_____ al baloncesto con unos amigos. El viernes por la noche mis hermanos
        9.

y yo _____ unos videojuegos nuevos. Mi papá _____ a las
            10.   **11.**

cartas con mis abuelos, y mis hermanitos _____ un juego de mesa muy
                                                      12.

divertido. ¿Y tú? ¿ _____ a un deporte la semana pasada?
                        13.

SCORE [   ]

Alternative Quiz 11-3A

C. Isabel plays soccer, tennis and volleyball, and is telling her grandmother about the results of some recent games. Complete their conversation with the correct preterite forms of **ganar.** (12 points)

ABUELA   ¿Qué tal el partido de fútbol? ¿Quiénes _____?

                                                          14.

ISABEL   Les _____ nosotros. ¡Fue un partido fabuloso!

                        15.

ABUELA   ¿Y el partido de tenis ayer? _____ tú, ¿verdad?

                                                   16.

ISABEL   No, no lo _____. Lo _____ mi amiga Dora. Ella

                              17.   **18.**

         juega muy bien.

ABUELA   Y cuéntame qué paso en el partido de voleibol el jueves. ¿ _____

                                                             19.

         ustedes?

ISABEL   Pues, no _____ nosotros, ni _____ el otro

                             20.   **21.**

         equipo. Fue un empate *(tie)*.

SCORE [   ]

TOTAL SCORE [/35]

12 Las vacaciones ideales

Alternative Quiz 12-1A

Maximum Score: 30

■ PRIMER PASO

Grammar and Vocabulary

A. Mauricio and Armando are talking about plans for after school. Complete their conversation with the Spanish equivalents for the English expressions. Remember that some Spanish verbs require **a** or **que** before the infinitive. (5 points)

MAURICIO ¿Qué 1. _____ hacer hoy después de clases?
                         (are we going)

ARMANDO Hace mucho calor, ¿no? 2. _____ ir a nadar. ¿Qué te parece?
                                      (I want)

MAURICIO ¡Perfecto! Pero sólo puedo nadar una hora. A las cuatro y media

            3. _____ estar en casa.
                   (I have to)

ARMANDO ¿Qué 4. _____ hacer en casa?
                      (do you need)

MAURICIO Pues, debo organizar mi cuarto. Oye, ¿5. _____ invitar a Rafa a
                                                        (are you going)

            ir con nosotros?

ARMANDO Sí, buena idea.   SCORE [   ]

B. This winter Sergio is going on a ski vacation, while his friend Ilsa is going to the Caribbean. Look at the lists of what they still have to get before leaving, then explain in Spanish what each person needs. Include the correct indefinite article. (10 points)

Sergio
6. jacket
7. ticket
8. camera
9. scarf
10. skis

Ilsa
11. towel
12. sunglasses
13. suitcase
14. sandals
15. bathing suit

Alternative Quiz 12-1A

6. _____   11. _____

7. _____   12. _____

8. _____   13. _____

9. _____   14. _____

10. _____   15. _____

SCORE _____

C. Victoria is describing her daily routine at school and home. Complete what she says with the correct present-tense form of the missing verbs. Some verbs may be used more than once. (15 points)

empezar	poder	venir	tener	almorzar	preferir

Las clases en mi colegio **16.** _____ a las ocho y cuarto. Siempre salgo para

el colegio a las siete y media porque **17.** _____ desayunar en la cafetería allí y

pasar el rato con mis amigos. Mi hermano Héctor es muy desorganizado y nunca

18. _____ tiempo para desayunar. Él y sus amigos **19.** _____

muchísima hambre todas las mañanas. Yo **20.** _____ a las once y media con

mis amigas. Típicamente nosotras **21.** _____ en la cafetería. Pero si hace

buen tiempo, **22.** _____ comer en el patio del colegio. Después de clases, a

veces mis amigas **23.** _____ a casa conmigo para mirar la televisión y pasar

el rato. Esta tarde ellas no **24.** _____ venir, porque todas nosotras

25. _____ que estudiar mucho para el examen de ciencias mañana.

SCORE _____

TOTAL SCORE _____ /30

Spanish 1 ¡Ven conmigo!, Chapter 12

12 Las vacaciones ideales

Alternative Quiz 12-2A

■ SEGUNDO PASO

Maximum Score: 35

Grammar and Vocabulary

A. Aurora and a friend are talking about what Aurora and her family would like to do on a dream vacation. Complete their conversation with the correct pronouns and forms of **gustar**. (10 points)

—Aurora, ¿a ti qué **1.** _____ **2.** _____ hacer para las vacaciones este año?

—A mí **3.** _____ **4.** _____ ir a América Latina. ¡A mis hermanos y a mí

5. _____ **6.** _____ escalar montañas en los Andes y explorar en la selva!

—¿Y a tus padres **7.** _____ **8.** _____ hacer esas cosas también?

—No, para nada. A mi madre **9.** _____ **10.** _____ hacer un viaje a

Europa y visitar todos los museos de arte. ¡Qué aburrido!

SCORE _____

B. A science magazine is interviewing Cecilia, a famous explorer and nature photographer. Complete the interview with the correct form of **ser** or **estar**. (16 points)

REVISTA   Buenos días y gracias por la entrevista. Cecilia, dime… ¿de dónde

     11. _____?

CECILIA   **12.** _____ de Venezuela, y todavía tengo una casa en Caracas.

     Pero no **13.** _____ allí casi nunca, porque

     14. _____ muy ocupada con mis viajes y mis videos.

REVISTA   ¿Y qué **15.** _____ haciendo estos días?

CECILIA   Un grupo de científicos *(scientists)* y yo **16.** _____ haciendo una

     película sobre el Río Amazonas.

REVISTA   Cecilia, viajas mucho y has visto *(you've seen)* muchos lugares. ¿Cuál

     17. _____ tu lugar favorito?

CECILIA   Los Andes, porque **18.** _____ tan altos y misteriosos.

REVISTA   Pues, Cecilia, gracias otra vez, y buena suerte con la película.

SCORE _____

Alternative Quiz 12-2A

C. Explain what each person or group is doing while on vacation. Use the correct form of the present progressive and a different verb for each sentence. (9 points)

mi familia y yo

19. _____

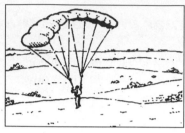

yo

20. _____

Lucinda

21. _____

tú y Hortensia

22. _____

mis primos

23. _____

Armando y Juan

24. _____

SCORE [   ]

TOTAL SCORE [   ] /35

CAPÍTULO 12

Spanish 1 ¡Ven conmigo!, Chapter 12

12 Las vacaciones ideales

■ TERCER PASO

Maximum Score: 35

Grammar and Vocabulary

A. Complete the sentences about what different people did in the countries they visited last summer. Use the correct preterite form of the verbs in parentheses and the Spanish names for the countries. (11 points)

—Diana **1.** _____ (explorar) Pekín, la capital de **2.** _____.
(China)

—Elisa, tú **3.** _____ (escalar) montañas y **4.** _____

(estudiar) italiano en **5.** _____, ¿verdad?
(Italy)

—José Ángel y Sofía **6.** _____ (sacar) muchas fotos de las pirámides en

7. _____.
(Egypt)

—Mis tíos **8.** _____ (visitar) muchos museos en **9.** _____.
(England)

—Yo **10.** _____ (caminar) por los bosques en **11.** _____.
(Germany)

SCORE ☐

B. Rosario's family is getting ready for a trip. Complete her statements and questions to her brother Suso about where everyone went while getting ready. Use the correct preterite forms of **ir.** (9 points)

12. Mamá y yo _____ al almacén para comprar ropa.

13. Luego, yo _____ a casa para hacer la maleta.

14. Geraldo _____ al centro comercial para buscar una maleta nueva.

15. Suso, tú ya _____ al banco, ¿verdad?

16. Después, tú y papá _____ a la librería para comprar un mapa, ¿no?

17. Y más tarde papá y Geraldo _____ al correo para comprar estampillas.

SCORE ☐

Alternative Quiz 12-3A

C. Juan and his friends stayed at home over summer vacation. Complete his conversation about what people did with the correct preterite forms of the verbs in parentheses. (15 points)

SOFÍA   Hola, Juan. ¿Qué tal las vacaciones? ¿**18.** _____ (Viajar) a algún lugar?

JUAN   No, pero yo lo **19.** _____ (pasar) muy bien aquí.

20. _____ (Trabajar) en un restaurante mexicano los fines de semana y **21.** _____ (jugar) al baloncesto en el parque todos los días.

SOFÍA   ¿Y tu amigo Héctor? ¿Él **22.** _____ (jugar) contigo?

JUAN   No, él **23.** _____ (tomar) unas clases este verano y

24. _____ (estudiar) para sus exámenes. Pero nosotros

25. _____ (hablar) por teléfono todos los días.

SOFÍA   ¿Qué más hicieron ustedes? ¿**26.** _____ (Nadar) en el lago mucho?

JUAN   No mucho, pero sí **27.** _____ (pescar) allí tres o cuatro veces.

SCORE [   ]

TOTAL SCORE [   ] /35

CAPÍTULO 12

Answer Key

Answers to Alternative Quizzes 1-1A, 1-2A, 1-3A

Alternative Quiz 1-1A

A. (9 points: 1 point per item)
1. días
2. mañana
3. Adiós
4. ¡Mucho
5. ¿Cómo
6. ¿Qué
7. Éste
8. señora
9. tú

B. (7 points: 1 point per item)
10. tú
11. yo
12. tú
13. yo
14. tú
15. yo
16. yo

C. (10 points: 2 points per item)
17. e
18. a
19. d
20. b
21. c

D. (9 points: 1 point per item)
22. me llamo
23. Encantada
24. Igualmente
25. estás
26. Estupenda
27. qué tal
28. Más o menos
29. Tengo que irme
30. Hasta luego

Alternative Quiz 1-2A

A. (10 points: 2 points per item)
1. es
2. es
3. eres
4. es
5. soy

B. (5 points: 1 point per item)
6. cómo
7. dónde

8. Cómo
9. cuántos
10. qué

C. (10 points: First two numbers .5 point each. Last number 1 point)
11. Dieciocho y siete son veinticinco.
12. Trece y nueve son veintidós.
13. Ocho y doce son veinte.
14. Veinte y tres son veintitrés.
15. Doce y seis son dieciocho.

D. (5 points: 1 point per item)
16. 459-2430
17. 235-1126
18. 791-1314
19. 846-1527
20. 367-1216

Alternative Quiz 1-3A

A. (15 points: 1.5 points per item)
Answers may vary. Possible answers:
1. la música pop
2. el jazz
3. el español
4. la clase de inglés
5. el baloncesto
6. el fútbol
7. la natación
8. el tenis
9. la ensalada
10. el chocolate

B. (8 points: 2 points per item)
11. ¿Te gusta la cafetería?
12. ¿Te gusta la clase de inglés?
13. Me gusta la comida italiana, pero me gusta más la comida china.
14. No me gusta la tarea.

C. (12 points: 1 point per item)
15. te
16. me
17. pero
18. no
19. Qué
20. mucho
21. gusta
22. más

Spanish 1 ¡Ven conmigo!, Chapter 1

Student Make-Up Assignments **151**

Answers to Alternative Quizzes 2-1A, 2-2A, 2-3A

Alternative Quiz 2-1A

A. (8 points: 1 point per item)
   1. tú
   2. Yo
   3. Yo
   4. Ella
   5. Él
   6. Ella
   7. Tú
   8. Él

B. (12 points: 2 points per item)
   9. unas carpetas
   10. unos papeles
   11. unas gomas
   12. unos libros
   13. unos lápices
   14. unos cuadernos

C. (8 points: 1 point per item)
   15. una; una
   16. una; un
   17. un; una
   18. una; un

D. (7 points: 1 point per item)
   19. una calculadora
   20. una mochila
   21. un diccionario
   22. un bolígrafo
   23. una carpeta
   24. papel
   25. una regla

Alternative Quiz 2-2A

A. (14 points: 2 points per item)
   1. Cuántas
   2. Cuántos
   3. Cuántas
   4. muchos
   5. muchas
   6. muchos
   7. mucha

B. (9 points: 1 point per item)
   8. cuarto
   9. una cama
   10. un armario
   11. un radio
   12. unos carteles
   13. ventanas
   14. una puerta
   15. una silla
   16. una lámpara

C. (12 points: 2 points per item)
   17. Hay dieciocho relojes.
   18. Hay veinticinco armarios.
   19. Hay veintiún escritorios.
   20. Hay doce camas.
   21. Hay quince televisores.
   22. Hay treinta mesas.

Alternative Quiz 2-3A

A. (8 points: 1 point per item)
   1. ciento noventa y nueve dólares
   2. ciento veintiún dólares
   3. treinta y ocho dólares
   4. cuarenta y siete dólares
   5. sesenta y cuatro dólares
   6. setenta y seis dólares
   7. ciento sesenta y cinco dólares
   8. cincuenta y tres dólares

B. (8 points: 1 point per item)
   9. a
   10. d
   11. g
   12. c
   13. e
   14. h
   15. f
   16. b

C. (9 points: 1 point per item)
   17. Quiero
   18. comprar muchas cosas
   19. necesitas
   20. quieres
   21. ir a la pizzería
   22. encontrar
   23. hacer la tarea
   24. organizar
   25. poner

D. (5 points: 1 point per item)
   26. ochenta y un
   27. treinta y una
   28. sesenta y siete
   29. veintiún
   30. veinticinco

Spanish 1 ¡Ven conmigo!, Chapter 2

Answers to Alternative Quizzes 3-1A, 3-2A, 3-3A

Alternative Quiz 3-1A

A. (12 points: 2 points per item)
1. Son las once menos cuarto.
2. Son las nueve menos cinco.
3. Es la una y veinticinco.
4. Son las diez menos veinte.
5. Es la una menos diez.
6. Son las ocho.

B. (8 points: 1 point per item)
7. inglés; arte
8. geografía; ciencias sociales
9. computación
10. matemáticas
11. ciencias; educación física

C. (15 points: 1.5 points per item)
12. la
13. los
14. las
15. las
16. Los
17. Las
18. la
19. el
20. los
21. las

Alternative Quiz 3-2A

A. (6 points: 1 point per item)
1. El televisor es del profesor Ibarra.
2. El libro de francés es de Sonia.
3. El reloj es de la profesora Cortez.
4. Las zapatillas de tenis son del director Muñoz.
5. La ropa es del estudiante nuevo.
6. La calculadora es de Ricardo.

B. (12 points: 1.5 points per item)
7. La clase de computación es a las ocho y veinte de la mañana.
8. La clase de inglés es a las doce y media de la tarde.
9. El almuerzo es a la una de la tarde.
10. El descanso es a las tres menos diez de la tarde.
11. El programa de televisión es a las cinco y media de la tarde.
12. La fiesta es a las nueve y cuarto de la noche.

13. El concierto de jazz es a las ocho menos cuarto de la noche.
14. La clase de matemáticas es a las diez y diez de la mañana.

C. (12 points: 2 points per item)
(15–20 Answers will vary.)

Alternative Quiz 3-3A

A. (7.5 points: 1.5 points per item)
1. Le gustan los deportes.
2. Te gustan los conciertos.
3. Le gustan los videojuegos.
4. Le gustan las fiestas.
5. Me gustan las novelas.

B. (7.5 points: 1.5 points per item)
6. A Rosaura le gusta el colegio, ¿verdad?/¿no?
7. A Rosaura le gustan los partidos, ¿verdad?/¿no?
8. A Rosaura le gustan los bailes, ¿verdad?/¿no?
9. A Rosaura le gustan las fiestas, ¿verdad?/¿no?
10. A Rosaura le gusta la comida china, ¿verdad?/¿no?

C. (12 points: 1.5 points per item)
11. La directora es simpática.
12. El colegio es pequeño.
13. La tarea es difícil.
14. La cafetería es bonita.
15. Los estudiantes son divertidos.
16. Las clases son buenas.
17. La profesora es alta.
18. El profesor es moreno.

D. (8 points: 1 point per item)
19. e
20. c
21. a
22. f
23. h
24. b
25. d
26. g

Answers to Alternative Quizzes 4-1A, 4-2A, 4-3A

Alternative Quiz 4-1A

A. (15 points: 1.5 points per item)
1. cuida
2. caminamos
3. lavan
4. mira
5. pasa
6. preparamos
7. descansa
8. tomo
9. hablo
10. haces

B. (10 points: 2 points per item)
Answers may vary. Possible answers:
11. A Juan Antonio le gusta nadar.
12. A Antonieta le gusta montar en bicicleta.
13. A mí me gusta tocar el piano.
14. A Marcelina le gusta pintar.
15. ¿Te gusta escuchar música?

C. (5 points: 1 point per item)
16. La persona que pinta es Lucía.
17. La persona que lava la ropa es don Francisco.
18. La persona que lava el carro es Sonia.
19. La persona que ve la televisión es doña Dora.
20. La persona que saca la basura es Toño.

D. (5 points: 1 point per item)
21. con él
22. con ella
23. conmigo
24. contigo
25. con ella

Alternative Quiz 4-2A

A. (12 points: 1.5 points per item)
1. Estás
2. estoy
3. estamos
4. Están
5. está
6. estoy
7. está
8. están

B. (14 points: 2 points per item)
Answers may vary. Possible answers:
9. Ellas están en la piscina.
10. Yo estoy en casa.
11. Él está en el supermercado.
12. Él está en el restaurante.
13. Ustedes están en el gimnasio.
14. Ellos están en la biblioteca.
15. Nosotros estamos en la tienda.

C. (9 points: 1.5 points per item)
16. Yo trabajo en un restaurante.
17. Nosotros pasamos el rato con amigos.
18. Él toca la guitarra.
19. Ella escucha música.
20. Ellos miran la televisión.
21. Ellas bailan con un grupo de baile.

Alternative Quiz 4-3A

A. (9 points: 1.5 points per item)
1. Los jueves
2. El sábado
3. Los fines de semana
4. El lunes
5. Los martes
6. El viernes

B. (9 points: 1.5 points per item)
7. voy
8. ir
9. vas
10. va
11. vamos
12. van

C. (12 points: 1.5 points per item)
Answers may vary. Possible answers:
13. Tú y Francisca van al gimnasio para tomar una clase de baile.
14. Mis amigos van a la tienda para comprar ropa.
15. Yo voy al parque para montar en bicicleta.
16. Víctor va a la piscina para nadar.
17. Papá va al supermercado para comprar comida.
18. Tú vas a la biblioteca para estudiar.
19. Mis amigos y yo vamos al café para tomar un refresco.
20. Beatriz y Marcela van al cine para ver una película.

Answers to Alternative Quizzes 5-1A, 5-2A, 5-3A

Alternative Quiz 5-1A

A. (5 points: 1 point per item)
1. Quiénes
2. Quién
3. Quiénes
4. Quién
5. quién

B. (8 points: 1 point per item) Some answers may vary. Possible answers:
6. durante la semana
7. con qué frecuencia
8. todos los días
9. siempre
10. muchas veces
11. a veces
12. sólo cuando
13. todavía

C. (9 points: 1.5 points per item) Answers may vary. Possible answers:
14. Nadie va con ella/Ella no va con nadie al centro comercial.
15. Nunca cuida/Ella no cuida nunca a su hermanita.
16. No quiere comprar nada para su cuarto.
17. Nadie camina con ella/Ella no camina con nadie en el parque.
18. Nunca estudia/No estudia nunca los fines de semana.
19. No necesita comprar nada para las clases.

D. (8 points: 1 point per item)
20. No/Nunca
21. nada
22. nunca/no
23. no/nunca
24. nadie
25. No/Nunca
26. nunca/no
27. nadie

Alternative Quiz 5-2A

A. (13 points: 1 point per item)
1. hace
2. Hacen
3. Leen
4. escriben
5. hacen
6. hago
7. corremos
8. asisto/asistimos
9. comen
10. como
11. bebo
12. come
13. bebe

B. (10 points: 2 points per item)
14. A ellos les gusta asistir al teatro.
15. A ella le gusta correr.
16. A ellos les gusta jugar al tenis.
17. A él le gusta bucear.
18. A ellas les gusta acampar.

C. (12 points: 2 points per item)
19. nos; comer
20. les; esquiar
21. les; pescar
22. me; recibir
23. le; leer
24. les; hacer ejercicio

Alternative Quiz 5-3A

A. (9 points: 1 point per item)
1. marzo
2. mayo
3. septiembre
4. enero
5. el invierno
6. agosto
7. meses
8. estación
9. la primavera

B. (14 points: 2 points per item)
10. El examen es el veintiuno de octubre.
11. La excursión es el treinta y uno de octubre.
12. La fiesta es el veintisiete de octubre.
13. El concierto es el cinco de noviembre.
14. El partido es el quince de octubre.
15. La cena es el veintidós de noviembre.
16. El baile es el primero de noviembre.

C. (12 points: 2 points per item) Answers may vary. Possible answers:
17. En Nueva York, hace fresco y está nublado.
18. En Miami, hace mucho calor y hace sol.
19. En Chicago, hace frío y hace viento.
20. En San Francisco, hace fresco y está lloviendo.
21. En Juneau, hace mucho frío y está nevando.
22. En San Antonio, hace calor y está lloviendo.

Answers to Alternative Quizzes 6-1A, 6-2A, 6-3A

Alternative Quiz 6-1A

A. (14 points: 2 points per item)
1. Mis padres
2. nuestra madre
3. mi madrastra
4. Sus hijos
5. mis hermanastros
6. Su padre
7. Nuestros perros

B. (10 points: 1 point per item)
8. tía
9. padre
10. primos
11. abuela
12. hermana
13. madre
14. hijo
15. esposa
16. abuelo
17. prima

C. (9 points: 1.5 points per item)
18. Geraldo
19. Pedro
20. María
21. Elisa
22. Clara
23. Pascual

Alternative Quiz 6-2A

A. (12 points: 1 point per item)
1. cómo son
2. listos/traviesos
3. mayor
4. menor
5. travieso/listo
6. De qué color es
7. pelirrojo
8. ojos
9. viejos
10. canas
11. se ve
12. atractiva

B. (8 points: 1 point per item)
13. traviesas
14. altos; delgados
15. pelirrojos
16. gorda

17. listos
18. jóvenes
19. atractivas

C. (6 points: 1 point per item)
20. X
21. a
22. X
23. a
24. a
25. X

D. (9 points: 1.5 points per item)
26. hacemos
27. hago
28. hace
29. salimos
30. salgo
31. salen

Alternative Quiz 6-3A

A. (6 points: 1 point per item)
1. pone
2. pongo
3. ponen
4. pone
5. ponemos
6. poner

B. (8 points: 1 point per item)
7. Debo
8. Debes
9. debemos
10. deben
11. debe
12. deben
13. debo
14. debemos

C. (16 points: 2 points per item)
15. debemos trabajar
16. Debo planchar
17. debe cuidar
18. deben poner
19. debes pasar
20. debo limpiar
21. debemos hacer
22. debe cortar

CAPÍTULO 6

Answers to Alternative Quizzes 7-1A, 7-2A, 7-3A

Alternative Quiz 7-1A

A. (10 points: 2 points per item)
1. Bartolomé viene del parque de atracciones.
2. Mamá y Papá vienen del campo.
3. Toño viene del circo.
4. Roberta y yo venimos de la fiesta de cumpleaños de su amiga.
5. Mis primos vienen del lago.

B. (12 points: 1.5 points per item)
6. empieza
7. prefiero
8. vienen
9. empiezan
10. preferimos
11. vienes
12. vengo
13. empezamos

C. (8 points: 1 point per item)
14. empiezas
15. prefieres
16. empieza
17. vienen
18. prefieren
19. empiezo
20. viene
21. preferimos

Alternative Quiz 7-2A

A. (9 points: 1.5 points per item)
1. afeitarse
2. maquillarse; maquillarte
3. lavarme
4. ducharte; ducharse

B. (10 points: 2 points per item)
5. afeitarme
6. lavarte los dientes
7. peinarte
8. maquillarse
9. ducharse

C. (7 points: 1 point per item)
10. Vas a ver
11. vamos a hacer
12. va a tener
13. Voy a ir

14. vamos a ver
15. va a ir
16. van a asistir

D. (9 points: 1.5 points per item)
17. piensas
18. piensan
19. piensa
20. pensamos
21. pienso
22. pensamos

Alternative Quiz 7-3A

A. (18 points: 2 points per item)
1. tiene que
2. tienen que
3. tienen prisa
4. tenemos ganas de
5. tienen ganas de
6. tiene que
7. tengo... prisa
8. tengo... sueño
9. tiene... años

B. (10 points: 2 points per item)
10. El profesor tiene ganas de ir al campo, pero tiene que trabajar.
11. Yo tengo ganas de ver una película, pero tengo que cuidar a mi hermanita.
12. Mis amigos y yo tenemos ganas de comer hamburguesas, pero tenemos que estudiar.
13. Tú tienes ganas de tomar un refresco, pero tienes que organizar tu cuarto.
14. Juan Domingo y Eufemia tienen ganas de asistir al baile, pero tienen que visitar a sus tíos.

C. (7 points: 1 point per item)
15. Te gustaría
16. tengo planes
17. Tal vez
18. lo siento
19. ocupado
20. cita
21. Qué lástima

Answers to Alternative Quizzes 8-1A, 8-2A, 8-3A

Alternative Quiz 8-1A

A. (5 points: 1 point per item)
1. almuerza
2. almuerzas
3. almorzamos
4. almuerzo
5. almuerzan

B. (4 points: 1 point per item)
6. podemos
7. pueden
8. puede
9. puedo

C. (16 points: 1 point per item)
Answers may vary for the verb.

10. me	18. me
11. encantan	19. encanta
12. me	20. le
13. gusta	21. gusta
14. me	22. le
15. gustan	23. gusta
16. te	24. le
17. gusta	25. gustan

D. (10 points: 1 point per item)
26. almuerzo
27. queso
28. papitas
29. sopa
30. plátano
31. toronja
32. fuertes
33. ligeros
34. cereal
35. pan tostado

Alternative Quiz 8-2A

A. (16 points: 2 points per item)

1. Son	5. están
2. son	6. Están
3. está	7. es
4. está	8. son

B. (8 points: 1 point per item)
9. picantes
10. saladas
11. fría
12. deliciosos
13. dulce
14. caliente

15. frío
16. deliciosa

C. (6 points: 1 point per item)
17. tiene sed
18. tienen sed
19. tengo hambre
20. tenemos hambre
21. tiene hambre
22. tienes hambre

Alternative Quiz 8-3A

A. (7 points: 1 point per item)
1. otros
2. otra
3. otro
4. otra
5. otras
6. otros
7. otro

B. (9 points: 1 point per item)
8. limpia
9. sucia
10. cuenta
11. Está incluida
12. vas a pedir
13. voy a pedir
14. Qué le puedo traer
15. Quisiera
16. Desea algo más

C. (12 points: 1.5 points per item)
17. quinientos noventa y un
18. ciento sesenta y ocho mil trescientas once
19. seiscientas cincuenta y cinco
20. treinta y seis mil setecientas cuarenta
21. ochocientos cuarenta y dos
22. once mil novecientos trece
23. dos mil ciento cuarenta y siete
24. cuatro mil ochocientos treinta y un

D. (7 points: 1 point per item)
25. una cuchara
26. un tenedor
27. una servilleta
28. un vaso
29. un plato hondo
30. un cuchillo
31. un plato

Spanish 1 ¡Ven conmigo!, Chapter 8

CAPÍTULO 8

Alternative Quiz 9-1A

A. (15 points: 1.5 points per item)
1. corbata
2. dulcería
3. tarjeta
4. joyería
5. tienda de comestibles
6. zapatería
7. pastelería
8. flores
9. juguetes
10. aretes

B. (12 points: 1 point per item)

11.	les	17.	me
12.	te	18.	nos
13.	les	19.	nos
14.	te	20.	me
15.	le	21.	me
16.	le	22.	nos

C. (8 points: 1 point per item)
23. cerca del
24. parque
25. lejos de
26. lejos de
27. a dos cuadras de
28. al lado del
29. a dos cuadras del
30. café

Alternative Quiz 9-2A

A. (10 points: 2 points per item) Answers may vary. Possible answers:
1. El almacén es más grande que la boutique.
2. La ropa en la Boutique Rosa es menos cara que la ropa en los Almacenes Peña.
3. Las personas que trabajan en el almacén son más simpáticas las personas que trabajan en la boutique.
4. La ropa formal en el almacén es tan elegante como la ropa formal en la boutique.
5. El almacén está menos cerca que la boutique.

B. (6 points: 1.5 points per item)
6. un traje rosa

7. un cinturón verde
8. un saco de cuadros
9. unos calcetines de rayas

C. (9 points: 1.5 points per item)
10. La cartera es de cuero.
11. Las botas son de cuero.
12. La corbata es de seda/lana/algodón.
13. Los calcetines de tenis son de algodón.
14. Los suéteres de esquí son de lana/algodón.
15. Las camisetas para niños son de algodón.

D. (10 points: 1 point per item)
16. unos bluejeans
17. unas sandalias
18. unos pantalones cortos
19. una camisa
20. una falda
21. una camiseta
22. una blusa
23. un traje de baño
24. unos zapatos
25. un suéter

Alternative Quiz 9-3A

A. (6 points: 1.5 points per item)

1.	barato/a	3.	caro/a
2.	¡Qué ganga!	4.	¡Es un robo!

B. (15 points: 1.5 points per item)

5.	Ese	10.	esta
6.	estas	11.	esos
7.	este	12.	este
8.	estas	13.	esas
9.	esas	14.	esa

C. (6 points: 1 point per item)

15.	cuesta	18.	cuesta
16.	cuestan	19.	cuesta
17.	cuestan	20.	cuestan

D. (8 points: 1 point per item)

21.	Cuánto cuestan	25.	prefiero
22.	cuesta	26.	me gusta más
23.	Cuál de	27.	Te queda
24.	la gris	28.	Además

C
A
P
Í
T
U
L
O

9

Answers to Alternative Quizzes 10-1A, 10-2A, 10-3A

Alternative Quiz 10-1A

A. (9 points: 1.5 points per item)
1. Estoy colgando
2. está decorando
3. qué te parece si
4. Me parece bien
5. Crees que
6. creo que no

B. (14 points: 2 points per item) Answers may vary. Possible answers:
7. estamos comiendo sándwiches
8. está organizando su cuarto
9. estoy leyendo el libro de españo
10. están poniendo la mesa
11. estamos haciendo la tarea
12. está buscando un regalo
13. están bebiendo agua

C. (12 points: 1 point per item)
14. el Día de los Enamorados
15. el Día de Acción de Gracias
16. el Día del Padre
17. el Día de Acción de Gracias
18. el Día de la Independencia/la Nochevieja
19. la Navidad
20. el Día de las Madres
21. el Día de la Independencia
22. la Nochevieja; el Año Nuevo
23. la Navidad
24. las Pascuas

Alternative Quiz 10-2A

A. (20 points: 2 points per item)
1. Prepara
2. Ayuda
3. Lava
4. Haz
5. Pon
6. Ve
7. Limpia
8. Cuida
9. Saca
10. Corta

B. (7 points: 1 point per item)
11. Perdóname
12. me haces el favor de
13. cómo no

14. me ayudas a
15. Lo siento
16. traes
17. un momentito

C. (8 points: 1 point per item) Answers may vary. Possible answers:
18. ¿Me pasas las decoraciones, por favor?
19. ¿Me ayudas a mandar las invitaciones, por favor?
20. ¿Me traes helado y galletas del supermercado, por favor?
21. ¿Me ayudas a limpiar la casa, por favor?
22. ¿Me ayudas a colgar los globos, por favor?
23. ¿Me ayudas a poner las sillas en la sala, por favor?
24. ¿Me ayudas a poner los regalos en el cuarto, por favor?
25. ¿Me ayudas a inflar los globos, por favor?

Alternative Quiz 10-3A

A. (15 points: 1.5 points per item)
1. celebramos
2. ayudamos/ayudaron
3. prepararon
4. hizo
5. decoraron
6. ayudó
7. invité
8. llegaron
9. cenamos
10. llamé

B. (10 points: 2 points per item)
11. Sí, lo corté.
12. Sí, lo ayudé.
13. Sí, ya la lavé.
14. No, no lo compré.
15. No, no lo limpié.

C. (5 points: 1 point per item)
1. ayer/anoche
2. Ayer
3. el sábado pasado
4. Anteayer
5. La semana pasada

Answers to Alternative Quizzes 11-1A, 11-2A, 11-3A

Alternative Quiz 11-1A

A. (12 points: 2 points per item)
1. me siento
2. te sientes
3. se sienten
4. nos sentimos
5. se sienten
6. se siente

B. (10 points: 1 point per item)

7. se	12. me
8. nos	13. se
9. te	14. se
10. te	15. te
11. se	16. te

C. (8 points: 2 points per item) Answers may vary. Possible answers:
17. Mis amigos y yo patinamos sobre ruedas en el parque.
18. La señora Soto hace yoga por las mañanas.
19. El señor Urrutia se estira en el gimnasio.
20. Micaela levanta pesas los fines de semana.

Alternative Quiz 11-2A

A. (14 points: 1 point per item)

1. nos	8. duele
2. duelen	9. me
3. les	10. duelen
4. duelen	11. le
5. le	12. duele
6. duele	13. me
7. te	14. duele

B. (9 points: 1.5 points per item) Answers may vary. Possible answers:
15. Tiene fiebre.
16. Está resfriado.
17. Estoy nervioso/a.
18. Tiene tos.
19. Tenemos gripe.
20. Tienen fiebre.

C. (12 points: 1.5 points per item)
21. cabeza
22. oídos
23. boca
24. ojos
25. manos
26. dedos
27. brazos
28. piernas

Alternative Quiz 11-3A

A. (14 points: 2 points per item)
1. fueron, canchas de fútbol
2. fue, estadio
3. fuimos, canchas de tenis
4. fui, pista de correr
5. fueron, parque
6. fuiste, piscina
7. fue, gimnasio

B. (9 points: 1.5 points per item)
8. jugamos
9. jugué
10. jugamos
11. jugó
12. jugaron
13. Jugaste

C. (12 points: 1.5 points per item)
14. ganaron
15. ganamos
16. Ganaste
17. gané
18. ganó
19. Ganaron
20. ganamos
21. ganó

CAPÍTULO 11

Answers to Alternative Quizzes 12-1A, 12-2A, 12-3A

Alternative Quiz 12-1A

A. (5 points: 1 point per item)
1. vamos a
2. quiero
3. tengo que
4. necesitas
5. vas a

B. (10 points: 1 point per item)
6. una chaqueta
7. un boleto
8. una cámara
9. una bufanda
10. unos esquís
11. una toalla
12. unos lentes de sol
13. una maleta
14. unas chancletas/sandalias
15. un traje de baño

C. (15 points: 1.5 points per item)
16. empiezan
17. puedo
18. tiene
19. tienen
20. almuerzo
21. almorzamos
22. preferimos
23. vienen
24. pueden
25. tenemos

Alternative Quiz 12-2A

A. (10 points: 1 point per item)
1. te
2. gustaría
3. me
4. gustaría
5. nos
6. gustaría
7. les
8. gustaría
9. le
10. gustaría

B. (16 points: 2 points per item)
11. eres
12. Soy
13. estoy
14. estoy
15. estás
16. estamos
17. es
18. son

C. (9 points: 1.5 points per item) Answers may vary. Possible answers:
19. Mi familia y yo estamos bajando el río en canoa.
20. Estoy saltando en paracaídas.
21. Lucinda está exploranda.
22. Tú y Hortensia están sacando fotos.
23. Mis primos están tomando el sol.
24. Armando y Juan están acampando.

Alternative Quiz 12-3A

A. (11 points: 1 point per item)
1. exploró
2. China
3. escalaste
4. estudiaste
5. Italia
6. sacaron
7. Egipto
8. visitaron
9. Inglaterra
10. caminé
11. Alemania

B. (9 points: 1.5 points per item)
12. fuimos
13. fui
14. fue
15. fuiste
16. fueron
17. fueron

C. (15 points: 1.5 points per item)
18. Viajaste
19. pasé
20. Trabajé
21. jugué
22. jugó
23. tomó
24. estudió
25. hablamos
26. Nadaron
27. pescamos

CAPÍTULO 12

DATE DUE

MAR 1 6 2005			

Demco, Inc. 38-293